Cami Earns
Her Ears

Cami Earns Her Ears

My Secret Walt Disney World Cast Member Diary

EARNING YOUR EARS: VOLUME SIX

Cami Scovotti

Theme Park Press

Editor: Bob McLain
Layout: Artisanal Text

ISBN 978-1-941500-53-8
Printed in the United States of America

Theme Park Press | **www.ThemeParkPress.com**
Address queries to bob@themeparkpress.com

Thank you, Mom and Dad, for supporting me both emotionally and financially throughout my entire college program, and to Becky and James for being my "adoptive Disney parents" and taking care of me during my time in Florida.

Contents

About "Earning Your Ears"

The "Earning Your Ears" series chronicles the experiences of young people from around the country and around the world who leave home, often for the first time, to live and work in Walt Disney World or Disneyland for several months, or even longer.

They are given "roles" to perform, from working in a Disney restaurant or shop to donning a costume and becoming one of the Disney characters who appear in the parks.

Each book in the EARS series makes you an honorary cast member as the author takes you behind Disney's pixie dust curtain to learn things the Mouse would prefer you didn't know, and what no guidebook will tell you, including how the theme parks operate from the inside out and what Disney employees do when they're not wishing you a magical day.

The EARS series currently includes six books, with a new volume published by Theme Park Press every few months:

- Amber Earns Her Ears
- Ema Earns Her Ears
- Sara Earns Her Ears
- Katie Earns Her Ears
- Brittany Earns Her Ears
- Cami Earns Her Ears

If you've ever wondered what it would be like not just to visit a Disney theme park but to work in one, the "Earning Your Ears" series is your E-ticket!

To learn about forthcoming books and everything there is to know about the Disney College Program, please visit us on Facebook:

Facebook.com/EarningYourEars

Foreword

I love publishing EARS books.

When I started the "Earning Yours Ears" series back in 2013, with *Amber Earns Her Ears*, I figured it would be a one-and-done. But Amber's book was not only popular, it was inspirational, too. Others who had taken (or were taking) the Disney College Program (DCP) wanted to share their experiences.

Not everyone, unfortunately, can write an EARS book. For every twenty pitches I receive, one makes the grade. What amazes me is the diversity: no two stories are alike. And what amazes me even more is the hope and the wonder and the potential that each DCP participant brings. Forget about the cynical accusations that Disney uses college program participants as low-wage labor. There's more to it.

Cami Scovotti, the author of this book, told her interviewer that she'd accept a role in Housekeeping. The interviewer was a bit surprised: Housekeeping is the least favorite role and involves the most work—plus the full-time Housekeeping cast members are notoriously nasty to college program temps. It didn't go well for Cami.

But she didn't "self-term", or voluntariliy leave the program, and instead got herself "recast" into a role at the Magic Kingdom. And there her adventure truly began, not so much at work, but back at her apartment, where roommate drama reached fever pitch.

No other EARS book that I've published reads so much like a pilot script for a new reality TV show. The cast of characters includes unstable co-workers, jilted suitors, and guests whose stories will bring tears to your eyes. Cami's story is equal parts pathos and pixie dust.

I publish EARS books because it feels good to publish EARS books. I don't sell a huge number of them. They do well, but the authors aren't relaxing on yachts. Most have gone on from their Disney experience to the real world of making grades in college and worrying about what kind of job awaits them and whether they'll be earning enough for a mortgage and what they really want to do with their lives.

For a few months, however, none of that matters. They're making minimum wage for menial labor in a sea of others doing the same thing. And they love it. It's their childhood dream come true. Whatever role Disney had played in their lives, they are now part of it. Like Amber and all the rest, Cami's on stage, as Disney likes to describe it, and making the same kind of magic that once was made for her.

So why, really, do I love publishing EARS books? If you read enough of them, you'll find life itself encapsulated: the uncertainty of whether you're good enough to make the cut, the transition from what you've known all your life to something new and quite grand, the settling in to work and friends and routine, the responsibility of being on your own and having others rely upon you, and finally, inevitably the winding down and the departure. All of this, in just a few months.

I could publish 100 EARS books and still not run out of unique tales about the Disney College Program.

Cami's story is one of them.

Bob McLain
Theme Park Press
August 3, 2015

Introduction

They tell you that the Disney College Program will change your life. They tell you that it is an "amazing resume-enhancing experience" and "a great opportunity to work with a Fortune 500 company for six magical months", but they leave out so much more.

When you get ready to jump into this experience you make your packing list, you find your roommates, you listen to your Disney playlist on repeat constantly just to get yourself through the waiting, but no matter what you do, no matter how much you prepare yourself, you're never quite ready for what this place has in store for you. You can't even begin to imagine the things you'll experience or the people you'll meet.

This is the program that will change your life.

This is the story about how it changed mine.

Chapter One

I first learned about the Disney College Program in the beginning of September 2013. My family and I had finally raised enough money to go on our first Disney Cruise, which was to sail out of Cape Canaveral on September 1. I boarded the ship as a Hospitality major, and I was very curious about the "hotel side" of the ship. I wanted to know how many rooms they had, how many housekeepers it took to turn over the rooms twice a day, and all of the work it took to make that famous magic behind the scenes.

I went to the Guest Relations desk and requested to meet with a Housekeeping manager to ask questions about the ship's operations. I was given a "maybe", but the next day they left a message in our cabin's voice mail with the news that I'd been scheduled for a meet and greet with the Guest Relations manager.

I asked this person for her advice in getting a foothold in the industry after graduation, and specifically about getting hired by the Disney company. She told me that she had started through the Disney College Program.

"I never would have dreamed of this," she said. "I was just a girl from a small farm town, and now I'm here as a leader at Disney Cruise Line. It's unbelievable, and I could not have done it without that program."

As soon as I got home, I started looking into the program. I saw that applications just so happened to be open and they were right in the middle of the recruiting season. "What could it hurt?" I thought, and so on the afternoon of September 16, I submitted my application.

At around 10pm that same night, I received the email saying that I had three days to take my web-based interview. I took it the very next day in my school's computer lab, and the second I hit submit the screen came up with the page telling me that I was a "strong candidate" and that I had another three days to schedule my phone interview.

At this point, I told all of my managers at the Marriott that I was applying for the program. I was lucky in the sense that I had 100% confidence and support from all of them. They each gave me great advice for my phone interview and gave me ideas for questions to ask. "Keep notes on your desk, you're going to be so nervous during the interview that you're going to forget some things, and you might get a little scattered" was what one of the managers, David, had told me. I'm glad he did, because those notes that I kept on my desk saved me.

My phone interview went poorly. I was so nervous that my brain went into this weird, "shut-down" state that I couldn't get out of. I went monotone, I had no enthusiasm in my voice, I was tripping over words and speaking slowly. I was absolutely nothing at all like myself.

At one point I even said "yes, ma'am" to my interviewer, who was undoubtedly male.

When he asked me how I handled emergencies, I explained the role I had played during the major flooding that had just hit Colorado the week before. He also asked me if I had really meant to put "moderate interest" under Housekeeping, since most applicants have no interest in housekeeping at all.

"Well, sure, my major is Hospitality and Hotel Management, and I know that if I want to be even a decent hotel manager I am going to have to know all of my hotel operations, especially housekeeping."

Apparently that was good enough for him, because on October 1 I received my acceptance email—for the role of Housekeeping.

I knew that my old car would not make the trip down to Florida. Rather than wait to see whether I *would* be accepted the program, and have to worry about making a trip down to Florida, I gambled and decided to buy a new car. I was on my way to sell my old car when I got the acceptance email from Disney—exactly 24 hours after I had bought the new one. I was relieved, to say the least. The old car was sold, the new car was ready to go, and I could not have been more excited to start this new adventure.

I created a Tumblr blog to record my experience and made a "room-mate survey video" to post both there and on the Facebook group for the College Program. The post on Tumblr brought me a response from Jessica, and we instantly agreed to be roommates. She told me that she already had agreed to room with two other girls, Kristen and a second Jessica (who I nicknamed "Legs" because that's how I thought her last name was pronounced when we first met).

We decided to get a three-bedroom apartment to cut down a bit more on rent, and began looking for two additional roommates. We met Erica on the Facebook page; she had a personality similar to Kristen's, and so the two of them chose to share one of the three bedrooms in the apartment. Soon thereafter we found Veronica, the final member of our little group, and the two of us decided to room together, leaving the two Jessicas to their own room.

Then the problems started.

Kristen posted on our group Facebook page that she couldn't stand any of us and that we were stressing her out because we loved Disney too much, and she did not. She decided to leave the group, and Erica found Kayla to replace her.

To this day, we still know nothing about Kayla. If we ever passed her on the street, we wouldn't recognize her. We often messaged her and texted her and she would never respond. To make matters worse, Erica became very controlling; she demanded that she be the first one in the apartment and that we were going to make a video blog, but we had to dress a certain way for the videos and use nicknames that she assigned to us (she just couldn't handle that we had 2 girls in the apartment named Jessica).

After short deliberation, the rest of us told Erica that we no longer wanted to be roommates with her or with Kayla. We wanted a good roommate experience. We were coming here to learn how to be independent, and having a controlling roommate was not part of the plan.

In the end, we decided to bag the idea of a three-bedroom apartment and stick with just the four of us: Veronica, the Jessicas, and myself.

I spent the following several weeks focused almost entirely on the program. I was hardly paying attention in my classes (which I do not recommend, by the way) because I was constantly talking to people on the Facebook group, talking to my roommates, constructing my bucket list, and looking up pictures of Walt Disney World.

My mom and I also spent a lot of time figuring out how to get me to Florida. It was no question that I was bringing my car. Originally, her and my grandmother were going to drive down with me. It wasn't until my mom's surgery was scheduled on our day of departure that plans had to change. We couldn't delay the trip, because she'd be recuperating. We thought about driving down two weeks early and I would stay with one of my future roommates until check-in day. We thought about me flying down and Mom driving the car down later. We thought of everything. Eventually, my grandfather called and offered to drive with me to Florida. He was going to be visiting us anyway around that time, and since he was a truck driver he knew the route from Colorado to Orlando quite well.

It worked out perfectly. I was ready to go, but still had my goodbyes to make—*long* goodbyes, as I did not plan on returning home to Colorado after my program. My best friend Megan and I got matching snowflake tattoos that were inspired by *Frozen*, we had a going-away party with the other banquet servers from the Marriott, and the little boy that I babysat told me that he would miss me a lot and asked when he would see me again. I didn't know what to say, so I told him a year.

"A year? Cami. That's 12 months. I don't think I can stand to be away from you that long. I better give you one hug for each month that you will be away from me."

Finally, on the morning of January 16, I said goodbye to my little brother as he left for school, and then my grandfather and I drove to the hospital to say goodbye to my mom. I felt terrible leaving her at the hospital to go through recovery without me there to take care of her, but with my grandmother at her (bed)side I knew she would be okay.

It took us three days to get to Orlando. We drove straight down through Texas, and then across Louisiana, Mississippi, and Alabama. We could not have asked for better weather or traffic. It was a smooth trip and it got us there a day early. So, on January 19, my grandfather and I went to Downtown Disney to look at all of the shops. I don't know who had more fun; he really enjoyed everything that he saw!

In one gift shop, I was looking for an Eeyore mug for my mom when he came up to me with a pressed penny that he had made in a machine "Here, I made this for you so you can remember our weekend together!" It was the sweetest thing my grandfather has ever done for me. My first real memory of Disney was when he and my grandmother took me to Disneyland as a kid, and now my first time at Walt Disney World was being spent with him, too.

We decided to sit in front of Splitsville for a drink. He got a beer and I got an Icee. We just sat outside and people watched for a few minutes, and I guess it really made him happy because he called my grandmother (who did not answer, because she constantly loses her phone) and left her a voice mail saying, "Hey! Susan! Guess what? It's January, 75 degrees outside, and I'm sitting at Disney World with my granddaughter drinking a beer. HAHA!" I would have loved to see her reaction upon hearing that voice mail, since she was still in Colorado buried in snow.

My friend Harrison who I had met on the Facebook page told me that he was also at Downtown Disney and wanted to meet up, so I invited him to join us at Splitsville. It was the first time that I had met him in person, and I thought he seemed nice enough. A little nerdy, I suppose, but in a good way. My grandfather and Harrison hit it right off. When Harrison mentioned the new Test Track ride, my grandfather was sold; I just sat back with my Icee and enjoyed the warm Florida weather while the two of them talked.

Later, my grandfather told me that "Harrison was a nice boy" and that "I should spend more time with him, invite him to dinner or something". I rolled my eyes and laughed. It wasn't that Harrison wasn't a nice kid, but I knew what my grandfather was up to. Getting me "married off" had been the mission of my family for months, and I was not about to go down that road.

My roommate Veronica and I were staying in the same hotel, so we drove back to Downtown Disney together—this time without my grandfather—to meet up with Jessica; her boyfriend, Adam (who was also in the program); and his roommates. We spent hours together talking and getting to know each other in front of the World of Disney, then we went to Adam's room at the Hilton to wait for his final roommate, Alec, to arrive, and played charades. Once Alec's taxi got to the hotel, we went out to Chili's for dinner. Alec and I seemed to have the most in common, since neither of us had been to Disney World before, and we promised to see Wishes for the first time together as soon as we could.

The next day, check-in day, was so packed with important events felt like a week rather than a single day. My roommates and I, along with Adam and his roommates, met up at the Starbucks across from Vista Way at six in the morning for coffee. We lined up outside of

Vista at exactly 7 am to start check in. While waiting in line we met new friends, and I ran into Samuel, who I had been talking to via the Facebook page for a few months.

During check in we found out that we were placed in a three-bedroom apartment and were going to be living with two other girls we hadn't even met. The news sparked a lot of anxiety, especially for Jessica and myself. We had worked so hard on our roommate group, and now we had to deal with two last-minute additions. Would they like us? Would we like them? As it turned out, the two newcomers were twins, Liz and Rachel, from New York, who were shy and less extroverted than the rest of us, but still very nice.

After we left the check-in station, we were sent on a bus to Casting. While waiting in line, I was approached by a man named Andrew, who asked me: "So, what's your role, Cami?" "Housekeeping" I told him, "at the All-Star resorts." This information seemed to excite him, and he began to tell me all about what I should expect.

"All-Star is a beast! Over 300 housekeepers check in there every morning, and you have to clean 18 rooms a day, 17 if they are all checkouts!" Everything he told me instantly made me feel overwhelmed, but I didn't want to show it; instead, I turned around the conversation.

"What's your role in the Disney show, Andrew?" He told me that he was a Housekeeping manager at Saratoga Springs. I was beyond thrilled with his answer. I immediately told him that my major in school was Hospitality with a concentration in Hotel Management, and I wanted to learn as much about hotels and resorts here as I could. I spent the next 15 minutes in line bombarding him with questions. Andrew started with the company through the College Program and loved what he did and wanted to help out incoming CPs. He wrote his email down in my program guide and told me that if I ever had any more questions, needed any help, or if my leaders were not supporting me, to let him know and he would be there for me. I couldn't believe that not even four hours into this program I was already networking.

Throughout the many lines that formed in the Casting building, I made friends with a nice boy named Bryan, who was a lifeguard at Port Orleans. When we were finally done with all the lines, we ran into Veronica and waited for the bus together. The bus to take you back to Vista Way will not let you on without first showing the driver your housing ID. Of course, between all of the papers, supplies, and bags they had given me throughout the day, I had already lost my ID. The bus was not going to wait for me, either. Luckily, Bryan and Veronica were nice enough to wait with me and helped me look through my three bags to get my ID. We traded phone numbers with Bryan, and invited him for dinner a few days later.

After check in, Jessica, Veronica, and I went to Target to get some initial shopping done. I talked to Samuel on the phone for half of the time that I was there, reminding him that I had brought a ficus tree with me from Colorado and that I needed help carrying it up the stairs.

As soon as we got home, Samuel came over and helped carry up the ficus. He brought his own lunch which he ate while we talked, and then he and I laid down on the living room floor and talked for hours. I had been talking to Samuel since October, and I thought he was damn near perfect. Now that I was meeting him in person, I was even more smitten. We had been constructing a list of things we were going to do together, the cupcakes we would eat, the rides we would ride. I was almost as excited about him as I was about everything else.

That night, all six of us, along with Samuel, walked across the street to Chatham to visit Adam and his roommates at their apartment. We played Apples to Apples and talked until around two in the morning. It made for a long day, but it was a great way to start the program. I was settled into a place to call home for a while with wonderful people that I enjoyed and already loved. There was no way of knowing what the rest of the program was going to hold for any of us, but for that first night we were all together and happy.

Chapter Two

Waiting for this program to start brought a lot of struggle,such as not being able to pay attention in class, my parents' being upset that their "baby is leaving them" , packing everything I own, and saying goodbye. One of the hardest things about waiting for the arrival date was anxiety about meeting my roommates in person. In the months before the program, they had become some of the best friends I have ever had, though all of our interactions were online and by phone. When we finally met each other, there was a lot of screaming and crying. I remember going to meet Jessica at Downtown Disney, seeing Adam first, screaming and then tackling Jessica underneath the spitting Stitch at World of Disney. Jessica kept saying, "You're real! You're actually real!"

The night after our arrival day, we had reservations to eat at Chef Mickey's in the Contemporary Resort. When we originally made the reservations, we still intended to room with Erica and Kayla, so the reservations were for six. Erica still wanted to come, since we all planned on going in "Disneybound" outfits (cute outfits that resemble Disney characters), and apparently she had spent a lot of money on hers. We hadn't spoken with Erica in over a month, and we'd all forgotten about her—right up until the day of the dinner.

That afternoon I had my housing meeting and then the "Housekeeping Town Hall" (which was just a Housekeeping support group). During those meetings, Erica had called and texted me almost a dozen times, asking if she was still invited, wanting to know where I was, and why I wasn't responding to her. I was annoyed when I looked at my phone, and instantly remembered why we had told her that we didn't want to live with her. I explained to her that Disney had assigned us a three-bedroom apartment after all, and that we had invited our new roommates, the twins, to eat with us so we could get to know them. That left no room for Erica on the reservation.

"I hope you understand," I texted.

"No. I don't understand. But quite frankly, I don't care anymore," she texted back. I didn't reply.

I continued walking home from the meeting at the Commons; it was a 20-minute walk back to our apartment at Patterson. When I approached the gate I noticed a girl leaning over the fence crying. I stopped to see if she was okay, and when she looked up I realized who it was. Erica.

"Are you Erica?"

"Yes."

"Are you okay?"

"I'm fine. Are you Cami?"

"Yeah..."

"Well, then, this is weird."

"Its not weird unless you make it that way, Erica."

"I'm making it that way"

"Alright, then, in which case I am walking away."

I really wasn't trying to be mean, but I was not in the mood to deal with it, and to be honest I was completely creeped out that she was just sitting in front of Patterson crying, especially since she did not live there. When I got home, I told Veronica, Jessica, and Legs what had just happened. Jessica just laughed and told me that the twins had told her not 5 minutes before that they didn't want to come to dinner with us—they were going out with their mom before she went back home. So, potentially, the entire situation with Erica could have been avoided, but this evening together was what the four of us really needed to celebrate the start of our programs, without any of the stress and awkwardness that Erica may have brought.

Once we got to the Contemporary, we went straight to the gift shop and bought our first autograph books and pens. Throughout dinner, we celebrated with Mickey, Minnie, Goofy, Donald, and Pluto. This was my first experience with Walt Disney World characters, and I was just beginning to learn how talented and, well, magical the character performers are. We had unique experiences with each character that I'll never forget.

When Mickey Mouse made it around to our table, we were so excited to see him that I blurted out: "Mickey! We work for you now! We're cast members!" Mickey patted me on the head and walked away from us, shaking his head back and forth. Jessica and I couldn't help but laugh that we had just gotten shamed by Mickey Mouse the first day into our program. He came back a few minutes later and shook each of our hands, and then he made a gesture with both fists and began to walk away. Jessica looked at me and, "I think he's praying for us." Mickey stopped in his tracks, looked at Jessica, nodded, and kept walking.

When we were done with dinner, none of us wanted to go home. Jessica suggested taking the monorail to the Polynesian and the Grand Floridian. I looked at her like a small child because I loved the idea so much, and then they all looked back at me in awe because they had just realized that I had never rode the monorail before. I swear to you I have never climbed stairs so fast in my life as I did that night going up to the monorail station. We were talking to the cast member who was manning the gates and explained to him that this was my first monorail ride. He was almost as excited for me as my roommates were. He even gave me a monorail sticker and a couple of monorail cards. The four of us had a monorail car to ourselves, which of course meant we took lots of pictures.

We went to the Polynesian first and walked around, deciding that we needed to go eat breakfast at 'Ohana at some point. We were lucky enough to get "lei'd" when we walked outside. The four of us were quite the sight at this point, dressed as princesses with Hawaiian leis.

We hopped back on the monorail bound for the Grand Floridian, was my favorite part of the night. The Hospitality major in me cried a little when we walked inside; my jaw dropped looking at the chandeliers. The detail astounded me. After we were done looking at the main building of the Grand Floridian, we walked down to the dock where the ferry boats take guests to the Magic Kingdom and back. The boats were done running for the night, so we just sat on the dock. We had a perfect view of Cinderella Castle, which was now in an array of pink, yellow, green, and blue colors since the park had closed. It was my first time seeing the castle; granted, it was far away, but just seeing it in the distance over the water was enough for me. Everything was so quiet—it was the most peaceful moment that I had experienced since leaving Colorado. I leaned up against a pole and just stared off at the castle. None of us were talking, so I assumed they were all taking it in the same way I was.

Next thing I knew, I heard sniffling, and felt hands latching on to the back of my shirt. I turned around and saw Legs sobbing a little, and leaning in for a hug. To be honest, this surprised me. In the months of talking to each other before we came down here, she was the only one to never join in on Google chat calls or Skype dates. Actually, I don't think any of us had heard her voice before we got here. One thing was for sure, though, we all somehow expected her to be, well, louder. The way she presented herself through text messages made it seem like she was an outgoing, crazy person. Since we had arrived, however, she was like a mouse. We barely heard her talk. We were actually starting to think that she didn't like us, so seeing her sobbing and latching to the back of my shirt was a surprise. She told us she was just so happy to be with us and she loved us so much. Instantly, we were all brought to tears and kept hugging each other. For all four of us, this was the moment that it became real. Standing on the dock of the Grand Floridian staring at Cinderella's Castle—it doesn't get more surreal than that, especially when you consider that not even a week before we were all just living in small towns dreaming of...this.

I will never forget that night. It meant so much to have them there and to know that we were in this together and we really did care and love each other. No matter what was to come during our programs, we had this moment. That's all that really mattered.

Chapter Three

With the preliminaries past, it was time to start training for our roles. Training for the other girls in the apartment was over in just a couple of days, but mine lasted well over a week and a half. The training process for Housekeeping was also much different than that for the other roles—it started off much later, and while it was more extensive, it did not include an "assessment". As I watched my roommates stress out about their assessments being tomorrow, I thought to myself, "I am constantly being assessed."

The Housekeeping Town Hall that I mentioned earlier was not actual training, but I should address it anyway because of its importance. The town hall was held at the Commons, directly after the housing meeting for our arrival group. Several of the Housekeeping leaders from different resorts came and shared their stories about how they started with the company and how they grew into management. I was surprised to learn how many of them had begun their careers in the College Program. Andrew, who I had met at the Casting building on check in day, was there, and I enjoyed hearing a little more of his story.

It was entertaining to see the different personalities of all the leaders. One leader told us that he had met his wife in the College Program and encouraged us to find our "happily ever after" because we were at the place where "dreams came true". The next leader advised, "Alright, enough of the cheesy nonsense. You're here to work, and if you don't show up to your job or call in all the time because you're a CP (College Program participant) and you think nobody cares, we will send you home. Find your happily ever after, or whatever, but remember that you are here to do a job". That was Marlene, who would end up to be one of my favorite leaders at All-Star.

For the rest of the town hall, they had us introduce ourselves, since "this is probably the last time you'll see each other unless you make friends now". Yes, housekeeping is a very lonely job. For the most part, you're working by yourself. You don't see anyone else during the day unless it's on a lunch break or one of you has time to go help the other at the end of the day.

I'm glad I attended the town hall. It made me feel a lot more comfortable about housekeeping (I was nervous about it before starting the program). And it was great making friends who were also in Housekeeping. After all, they were the only ones who really understood just how hard you were working and understood exactly how annoying hair was and how you had developed a newfound hate for bobby pins.

Our first official day of training was an eight-hour long class held at Disney University titled Housekeeping Core. The instructor started out the class all sunshine and smiles. She introduced herself and got us warmed up with jumping jacks and introductions. "Let's watch a cute video about housekeeping!" she smiled as she turned on a video that showed Mary Poppins singing "A Spoonful of Sugar" and various video clips of Disney characters from different movies cleaning.

When the movie ended she asked us, "So, how did the video make housekeeping look?! It's FUN, right! Yes! Fun!" Her expression seemed to change instantly. "Now we're going to look at what housekeeping really looks like." She played a much less cheery video of a housekeeper cleaning a room. "Housekeeping is hard work," she told us, "and for some of you, this is going to be one of the hardest jobs you will ever have."

She was very serious, but she had a personal story to back up almost every point that she made throughout the day. Stories about needles, bed bugs, animals in the room. The hardest story she told was that some people come to Walt Disney World with the intention of dying. For a lot of people, this place is their last dying wish. They make a trip here with their kids and grandkids, and then die in their resorts at night in their sleep. It happens more often than we imagine. We had to be trained on what to do if we found a dead body in a room.

That, I decided, was my new worst nightmare about housekeeping.

Disney University has an entire classroom dedicated to Housekeeping training, full of every type of bed offered on Disney property and four bathrooms. We each had to take a turn cleaning bathrooms and making beds, in our dressed-up professional attire. I was thankful that I chose NOT to wear heels that day.

The second day of training was Resort Orientation. At All-Star they call it "Rolling Out the Red Carpet". We weren't just training with housekeepers, but with new hires for different positions across every line of business. We were given lots of safety topics and forced to partake in cheesy safety demonstrations "with a new buddy". Mine was an ICP (International College Program participant) from Australia, Jamie, who would be working at the concierge desk.

After our safety exercises, we were taught about the history of the resort and learned some interesting facts. For instance, in All-Star Movies the hockey sticks that line the buildings in the Mighty Ducks section each weigh over 2,000 lbs, and there are 101 Dalmatians across the two Dalmatians buildings. You could stand outside and count them, if you didn't believe it. We took a group photo and then walked across different portions of all three themes in All-Star (Music, Movies, and Sports). When we returned to the classroom, we were each given a copy of our group photo and an All-Star Resorts lunch box. When all the teaching was over, we were given our official training schedules.

Hands-on training was…rough. I did not have a good training experience. I didn't know what to expect going into it. I suppose I had figured that it would be like the experience I had with the housekeepers back home who were all from Mexico, but had taught me enough Spanish that I could effectively communicate with them. It was different here. Thee majority of the housekeepers were Haitian, and I had no idea how to communicate with them. My trainer's name was Taina and she spoke English, but only when she wanted to. I would try to talk to her and ask her questions about herself and she would either ignore me and start yelling at one of her friends, or she would just start singing very loud and ignore everything I had to say.

Taina explained that I would watch her for the first few rooms to see how she did things. After lunch, I was to make all of the beds and then the next day I would clean all of the bathrooms. My third day with her we would trade between beds and bathrooms for each room, but I would have to clean at least one room by myself. It sounded like a fair plan, except that she assumed I had learned everything in the Housekeeping Core class and did not want to teach me anything or answer my questions. Then, after lunch on the first day, she asked if she could borrow my phone. I unlocked it and handed it to her. She was on the phone for three hours and spent the entire time screaming, literally screaming, in her native language to whoever was on the other line and ignored me the entire rest of the day. She even neglected to mention that I was not allowed to clock out until 4:30, so when I clocked out at 4:00 and we returned to base, I got lectured by just about everyone in near proximity.

Interestingly enough, Taina wasn't at work on what was supposed to be my third day with her, so I was placed with another trainer, Pierre, who was nice but talked too much. He didn't care about how well my rooms were being cleaned, he just wanted to ask me about Colorado, what kind of music I listened to, and if I thought he would make a good manager. It was a pleasant change working with someone who was friendly, but the end of my day with Pierre marked the end of my training with another person. I was now on my own and did not feel prepared.

I met the other CP housekeepers at base the next morning, and we were all terrified about being on our own for the first time. We had packed our All-Star lunch boxes full of snacks and water because we were worried about not having the time to take a lunch break.

On the first day of ramp-ups, they give us 9 rooms to clean on our own; after that, it's 11, and then 13, 15, 17, and finally 18. We were ultimately required to clean 18 rooms per day as a Housekeeping cast member, and the ramp-up process was how Disney prepared you for it. The first day of 9 rooms wasn't terrible. It's a shock, however, going from cleaning rooms with another person to doing it by yourself, because you realize that it actually takes twice as long to clean the room as you had thought. Throughout ramp-ups you have to find your own routine for cleaning and discover which way of doing things is fastest for you. That's mostly what the first day is for.

At the end of my first day, when I went to turn in my key and my board to my leaders, I met Wyatt standing outside of the office. I had seen him around several times, knew that he was a CP, and was dying to talk to him. To be honest, I just wanted to be able to talk to *somebody* here. All the other CPs were located at Music, so meeting Wyatt was like an answered prayer. He had started the program a week before I did, and was on his 15-room ramp-up day (compared to my 9-room first ramp-up day). Wyatt was really smart, that wasn't hard to figure out, but I was surprised by how observant he was. He knew a lot more about me than I would have guessed, for someone who had never talked to me before. We were talking about cars, and I told him, "I drive a Kia Soul. Hamster car." He said: "I know. I watched you and your friends load up in your car after work yesterday and I made fun of you for driving a Kia." I was a little irritated that he was making fun of me when he didn't know me at all, but I was so thankful to have another CP to talk to that I let it slide.

On my third day of ramp-ups, I was given 13 rooms to clean, with 9 of them check outs. I was so overwhelmed when I saw my board. One of the housekeepers who liked to talk to me, a Jamaican named Opalyn, sat next to me on the Pargo that morning as we headed to the resort. She looked at my board and said, "Oh, baby. This is a hard board. Are you sure you can manage?" I told her I was going to try my best, but she just shook her head. I ended up being over an hour late to finish work that day, I hadn't yet figured out how to do that many check outs that fast, and none of the other housekeepers were willing to stay and help me finish my rooms. My leader, Keven, finally came to the room that I was cleaning at 5:30 and helped me finish and then gave the rest of the rooms to the PM shift. I was upset and embarrassed. Keven told me that I was fine for now, but I can't keep being late if I wanted to keep my job.

That was the first time I went home and cried after work. I sat on the floor in my bedroom and called my parents, and I just couldn't stop crying. I had done so well at not getting emotional or crying about anything through the entire two weeks that I had been in Florida, but the dam had broke and I couldn't stop the waterworks. "I'm just so tired," I kept telling my mom. "I was not expecting house-keeping to be so hard. What if I can't get myself to be fast enough? They're going to fire me and send me home!" I was such a mess. It didn't stop, either. For the first week on my own, I would come home and cry and sleep. I didn't even eat for that first week; I was too tired to cook. One day I got home at 5:00, fell asleep at 5:15, and didn't wake up until 7:30 the next morning to go to work. I was that tired.

The week gradually got better. One of my leaders, Lon, inspected the rooms that I had cleaned and assessed me on them. Usually, he would just say, "I don't really have anything bad to say. There was a thing here and there, but overall good job."

One day I asked Lon what exactly he was looking for when he went into a room and how assessments were scored. He said that once a week we get things called QA Assessments (QA meaning Quality

Assurance). The QA people went to every resort on Disney property and inspected every single room to make sure they all met company standards. They would assess one room from each housekeeper per month, and would grade that housekeeper. Essentially, when they went into a room they were looking for things that research showed our guests were looking for when *they* went into a room—clean mirrors, vacuumed floors, no cobwebs in the corners, the presence of a Bible in the night stand drawer and whether it had been vandalized by previous guests, what the beds looked like when they were made, and so forth. Each thing they looked for had a point value, and you were given a percentage score based on how many points you lost.

The next time that I worked with Wyatt was when we had our morning meeting for Movies. At this twice-weekly meeting, all of the housekeepers and leaders for Movies would come together and the leaders would deliver a safety message, translated in English, Spanish, and Creole, reminding us of things to do throughout the week (like what the beds are supposed to be like, what numbers to punch when you get into the room, etc). I sat down next to Wyatt, exhausted and defeated by my job, and proposed that we form a team.

"We need to start working together. Let's make a deal—whoever finishes first at the end of the day goes and finds the other one, and we help each other. Nobody gets left behind"

Wyatt just laughed.

"What is so funny?"

"Nothing. No, you're right, it's a good idea. They don't really tell you this, but I've noticed it—the Haitians help each other, and the Puerto Rican's help each other, but I haven't seen them help anyone outside of their group. It's a good idea. We should help each other."

We traded phone numbers and started our alliance. I was just slightly relieved; at least I knew that I would have help from here on out.

After work when everyone returned to the base building would be the only time I would see the other CP housekeepers, since they had all been placed in All-Star Music. Ashlee and Ilise had it the worst, and they were getting more and more upset every time we would meet back at base. It just wasn't getting any easier for them. Travis, with whom I had been extremely competitive since the first day we met at Housekeeping Core, had finally admitted defeat. He was exhausted and couldn't believe how hard housekeeping actually was. After his three days of hands-on training, All-Star made him a PM houseperson, which meant that he just drove the Pargos at night delivering objects to guests and occasionally cleaning a room if he had the spare time to do so. He really enjoyed it and did well at it. I would still see Travis at base after work, though he would be clocking in as I was clocking out.

My last day of ramp-up training—and the first day I had 18 rooms to clean—was by far the hardest. Not only didn't I have time for a lunch break, I had forgotten my water bottle at home. I came dangerously close to having an asthma attack and had to keep stopping to catch my breath. Wyatt was off, so I couldn't ask him to come help. But I was determined. I needed to prove to Keven that I could keep up. I finished my rooms right around 4:15pm. I was exhausted when I turned in my board, but I was glad to have completed the day. At this point, too, I was irritated with seeing the red "Earning my Ears" ribbon under my name tag. All of my roommates had theirs off for at least a week already.

"Hey, Keven, when do I get to take my ribbon off?"

"How many rooms did you clean today?"

"18."

"Then right now, I guess."

I swear to you that ribbon came off quickly. I was so glad that my training had finally ended. I even went to Epcot the next day and got an "I'm Celebrating!" button and wore it around for the day. I told myself that I was going to make it, despite the difficulties. I didn't want to go home, but I had made the decision to go to Health Services and submit a medical accommodation request to get recasted into a new role.

The process to get a medical restriction took weeks. When I first went to Health Services to submit the paperwork, they told me to call back in a week. When a week went by, I called only to be told that they had missed getting a signature from me on one of the papers and I needed to come back in and sign it before they could take it any further.

At this point, I was starting to get used to housekeeping. Wyatt and I had worked out a system of helping each other that was like clockwork. Wyatt had it down to a science. We would spend the morning Pargo rides constructing a plan for the day that would get us through our rooms the fastest. We figured out who was better and faster at what (Wyatt was usually better and faster at just about everything, but he never complained).

We started spending more time together outside of work, too. Wyatt was a proper gentleman. He was the type of guy that I always had hoped existed, but never actually met. One night we went to Downtown Disney and he took me to dinner at Planet Hollywood (my first time there). He told me about himself and his life in Kentucky— turns out he used to work in a coal mine before he came here. He told me about how much he loved his girlfriend, Taylor, and said that he wanted to marry her someday. Wyatt was an intriguing person. He was smart enough that everyone who met him believed that he could be running NASA someday if he wanted, yet he believed in certain fantasy things and wasn't afraid to talk about it. He was beautiful, in a way. Not to mention, he absolutely loved Katy Perry. At one point we were walking through Downtown Disney when I had to use the bathroom. I came out and found him sitting on a ledge:

"Sit down for a second. I want to talk to you."

My heart stopped. 'Here it comes,' I thought. 'He's going to tell me I'm annoying or he doesn't want to keep helping me with work or something.' I was worried about what he might say. Reluctantly, I sat down next to him.

"What do you notice?"

"About what?"

"Look around you. What do you notice?"

I looked around, trying to see anything out of the ordinary that he might be referring to, but I couldn't see anything. It looked like a normal evening at Downtown Disney. A few families, the occasional couple walking by holding hands, a group of college-age kids laughing (and who were more than likely other CPs). The lights in the trees were twinkling as always and little kids were playing and getting excited to be spat on by the Stitch that hung above the World of Disney entrance.

"Everything looks normal," I told him.

"Sure. But when you look around what's the first thing you *notice*?"

I really didn't know where he was going at with all of this, so I pointed out an older woman who was sitting by herself. He kept asking me questions about it: "Why do you think she's by herself?" "Who do you think she's waiting for?" "Why is she waiting for them?"

"Wyatt, what are you getting at?"

"Oh, nothing. I just want to know how your mind works." With that he stood up and started walking. He did things like that all the time. I never really understood why he did it; maybe it really was his way of trying to figure out how my mind worked, since I was shy about telling him details about my life, but it was still strange. I had never met anyone like him.

That night at Downtown Disney I was making myself so worried that I began to feel sick. I knew that the next day we had over 3,000 check outs happening at the All-Star. Every housekeeper was guaranteed to have 17 check outs on their board. I had never had that many and I was so afraid of being there too late that I was going to get some sort of coaching from our leaders. Wyatt promised that he wouldn't leave me behind. Don't get me wrong, I was beyond embarrassed admitting how dependent on him I had become, but it was all I could do.

The next day we made it through our full boards of check outs like champions. Wyatt kept texting me every few hours with messages like, "How are your rooms doing? Just checking in on you. You can do this!" His encouragement got me through the day and I was able to finish my board on time. After that I decided that if this was supposedly the worst of days, then maybe I'd stay a housekeeper if Health Services denied my case. With Wyatt and I working as a team, I knew I would be able to survive.

Chapter Four

By this time, my roommates had all finished their training. Some of us went to Magic Kingdom to celebrate, not too long before Valentine's Day. We were visiting Rapunzel, who noticed Jessica's Celebrating button, and asked what it was for.

"We earned our ears!" Jessica said

Rapunzel snarled through her teeth, not looking up from the autograph book, with a very forced, "Doing what?"

Now, in Jessica's defense, every other character we met that day stayed in their role and always asked with a cute, "Now what does that mean? It looks to me like you have ears already!" So when Jessica responded with, "Well, it means that we finished our training, we're official cast members now," she was just playing along to the story.

"I know what it means," Rapunzel snapped, slamming the autograph book shut with a heavy sigh "I swear everyone this week is either or a cheerleader or they're earning their ears."

Jessica and I looked at each other in an unsure way; clearly, Rapunzel didn't get her helping of pixie dust that morning.

Before we left I said, "Wait, will Flynn be here on Valentine's Day?"

She sighed again, "Yes. But only in the morning."

Jessica said, "Wait, only in the morning? He won't be here in the evening this year?"

Rapunzel rolled her eyes. "Yes. Only in the morning, and for reasons that I can't explain to you. Now you need to leave." Rapunzel grabbed Jessica and I each by a shoulder and pushed us out of her area toward Cinderella.

Jessica and I didn't know what to do. Looking back, I wish I had told an entertainment manager what happened. I have never had such a terrible interaction with a character, before or since. Jessica was so upset that she didn't want to see anyone else for the rest of the day. I didn't go see Rapunzel again for a while, either. It killed the experience for me.

All cast members need to keep this in mind, not just character performers: Disney, above anything else, is considered to be a magical place. There's an expectation that guests have when they come in and meet the cast members and the characters and experience the shows. The one rude princess could break a child's heart, the one "love and shove" Elsa could dishearten the family that waited hour hours to see her. The cast member working a parade who screams and gets in a guest's face could ruin the memories of that parade forever. As cast members, it's hard to preserve the magic when you're working out in the sun and humidity for 12 hours a day with guests who either don't listen or don't speak English. It gets frustrating, but we have to remember who we are and why we're here: To create magic for the guests, for the children of all ages. If you're a cast member, or about to be, and you're reading this, just remember that for me.

Meanwhile, back at the All-Star, we got a new leader. Lon was switched to be a leader for front desk at All-Star Music, and in exchange we got Michael. Michael started out his "Disney Story" with the College Program years ago. It was great having someone who understood what I was going through. He was the only leader I had met who seemed genuinely interested in talking to me. He wanted to know how I was doing with the program, if my roommates and I were getting along, what I was struggling with, if I was overall doing okay. Just him having the conversation with me meant so much. For the first time I felt like someone in leadership sincerely cared and it made me feel more comfortable being there.

I remember that neither Lon nor Keven had ever formally introduced themselves to me. I would see them when they came in to check on me and my trainer, but they never seemed interested in having a conversation. I had to ask Keven specifically to set aside a time when both him and Lon could meet with me so I could introduce myself to them and let them know my goals with the company. I tried to make sure they knew that my major in school was Hotel Management and I wanted to learn as much as I could from them while I was there. I don't recall now exactly what they said to me, but I do remember leaving their office feeling discouraged and worried that I wouldn't learn anything during my time in the program except for how to clean rooms. Having Michael as a new leader turned that feeling around.

But then things started to get weird with the roommates. I was becoming irritated with Veronica (the girl who shared my bedroom) and her constant sneaking out in the middle of the night to go drink at Vista Way, and then bringing weird boys into the apartment that she had just met. I tried hard to be patient with her, but she was starting to get overbearing, like a mom. The night that I went to Downtown Disney with Wyatt she called and demanded to know why I wasn't home yet, and when I did get home she was sitting at the kitchen table, clearly upset, and wanted to know what I was doing out so late. It made me mad that she treated me that way. I came out here to be independent, not to have another mom following me around.

I finally snapped when we went to the Magic Kingdom with the twins one day. She started pulling at my clothes, trying to make them look better. "Veronica! I look fine! Stop touching me and leave me alone!" It must have hurt her feelings, because she didn't talk the rest of the day. When we got home, we were greeted with the giant yellow paper sitting on the kitchen counter telling us that we had been inspected. Everything was fine for the most part, but the inspectors wrote the word "almost" next to the "failed" slot. Veronica was so angry she started stomping around the house and slamming doors.

"Veronica, what are you so upset about right now?"

"We almost failed inspections!"

"But we didn't. Veronica, its fine. We're not in trouble for anything, we aren't being fined anything, we still passed. Relax."

Veronica sat at her computer and plugged in her headphones and ignored me, which immediately sent me into a defensive mood. I don't respond well to people shutting me out instead of communicating. It lasted for 3 days. Legs and I were together almost constantly those three days, and Jessica and Veronica were together. The twins were still the twins, and kept to themselves. Legs and I were started to believe that Veronica and Jessica were mad at us. Veronica wasn't talking, Jessica was cancelling her plans with Legs, our roommate love note had been ripped off the fridge, and Veronica had taken all of my things and piled them on top of my bed. I was not happy.

Finally, on Valentine's Day I decided it needed to come to an end. The morning I took to myself. After all, I knew that Valentine's Day would be one of my only opportunities to meet the princes, and meeting Prince Phillip was the real dream. I put on my cutest dress and got to Magic Kingdom when it opened, just in time to see the welcome show (for the first time). As soon as the gates were open I ran straight to Fantasyland. I stopped at Castle Couture and asked to be covered in pixie dust (I was meeting royalty after all; I had to look my best). I got into Cinderella and Aurora's line first, saying a quick good morning to Cinderella and Prince Charming, and then moving quickly to Aurora and Phillip. They walked up to me and I froze, star struck, I suppose. (To future CPs or cast members: It's okay to be excited about character meet and greets. Keep that magic alive for yourself; it's worth it). When Phillip held my hands and told me that I looked stunning, I swooned. He was everything I wanted in a prince, especially when he asked where my prince was and I responded, "Well, you know, maybe." Then in unison Phillip and I both said, "Someday my prince will come." Aurora added, "Or perhaps you've already met him!" And again, in unison, this time the three of us: "Once upon a dream!"

The rest of the morning hardly mattered. Sure, I met Flynn Ryder and Snow White, and even Aladdin and Jasmine, Tiana and Naveen, and then Gaston, who told me that he would be my Valentine, since we were both single and very cute. After meeting everyone, I got a Dole Whip and sat next to the Partners statue. I watched propose in front of the castle. It was right about then that the singles awareness syndrome was kicking in, so I went home and prepared for the evening.

Legs, the twins, and I were throwing a party at our apartment. We made a whole bunch of cookies and then posted on the Facebook group that everyone was invited to come hang out with us and meet new people. We had probably 10 people or so show up, and we all just sat around the living room and talked about our roles and everything that we had to deal with. I was happy that one of the girls who came over was also a housekeeper;s she was the only one who really knew what I was going through.

At some point during the night, Jessica and Veronica came home and both went straight to their rooms. Angry, I walked right into Jessica's room. "What's going on? Did we do something to you guys? Why are you guys avoiding me and Legs?" Jessica explained that she thought that we were mad at them this entire time and were just as upset. That's when I decided that maybe I should work on my communications skills. I sat back down in the living room because Jessica announced that she and Veronica were going to Buffalo Wild Wings with Adam. When they came back home I was in the shower. Veronica came in to the bathroom shouting, "I got you a present! I got you a present!" I laughed and told her to get out of the bathroom. When I stepped out of the shower she gave me a little princess towel that she had gotten me and we both apologized.

We had survived our first roommate fight. Not that it was a legitimate fight, but we grew closer because of it and learned the importance of communicating our feelings to each other. I guess that's the key to any roommate situation, really, just a lot of communication. We knew it was going to be a struggle living with six girls for the entire program, and that learning how to deal with each other's personalities (some passive, some strong) was all a part of it.

We did overcome the differences, at least for a while, and as I got a little more used to housekeeping, I started taking the initiative to go out and do things more often.

Every Wednesday night, Buffalo Wild Wings turns itself into a karaoke bar/nightclub for cast members. Veronica, Legs, and I decided that we would go to check it out. It was a lot of fun, but the crowd was different than I had expected. On the dance floor, located on the outdoor patio, people everywhere were dancing (but not just dancing—they were acting completely trashy and wearing next to no clothing). Drinks were being spilled on people, people were getting burnt from cigarettes carried by other people who were trying to move through the crowd. In the bathroom there were girls throwing up and laying on the floor. I was amazed. Didn't these people realize that we were at a wing place, not an actual night club? Regardless, the three of us tried to make the most of it, after spending the money on the cover to get in. We danced for a couple of hours and occasionally stopped to talk to people that we knew from work or our classes.

One such person I ran into when I was fighting the crowd at the bar just to get some water. It was Jamie, the ICP that I had met during "Rolling Out the Red Carpet". He offered to get my roommates and I water, so we stood by a table while he fought the bar crowd for us. When he returned I introduced him to my roommates, who were clearly trying to hold back their laughter. They knew very well who Jamie was, because when All-Star had given us a copy of our group photo, I had pointed him out to them and said that he had introduced himself to the training group as "Jamie, from Australia, whose favorite movie was *Tarzan* because he was kind of a monkey himself." The funny thing was, he almost did look like a monkey.

Jamie hung out with us until Buffalo Wild Wings closed at 2am and kicked everyone out at the same time. I offered Jamie a ride home, since he didn't have a car, but he threw out the idea of not going home and going on an adventure instead. Legs, Veronica, and I looked at each other and shrugged. "Why not? Where do you guys want to go?" Jamie was already in the back seat of my car. "Let's just drive!" I got in, Legs was in the front seat. We were all quiet for a minute thinking of what to do when an idea sparked. I looked at Legs: "Do you want to go to the beach?" She said, "Yes, can we please?". I told her to GPS the closest beach and she told me there was one two hours away. "Great. Let's do it," I said and I turned on the car. It wasn't even before I got out of the parking lot when all three of us girls had to pee, so I pulled into the nearby McDonald's. Apparently, everybody who was at Buffalo Wild Wings had decided to go to McDonald's, because when I walked in there were drunk people everywhere.

One girl grabbed me by the shoulders and said, "Listen, listen to me... where do you work?"

"All-Star Movies"

"Oh, thank GOD," she said, wrapping her arms around my shoulders and whispering in my ear, "I work at Magic Kingdom and it SUCKS DICK." She then fell backwards, on top of two guys who were sitting atop a table next to us. She started talking to one of them and I looked at him and asked, "Is she with you?"

"No, I thought she was with you. I don't know anything about her."

The girl stood up and began to walk away, turning around long enough to yell, "I work at Magic Kingdom!"

"She works at Magic Kingdom," I said to the guys sitting on the table "That's all I know about her." They just laughed and I introduced myself to them and talked while I waited for the rest of my group to be ready. When everyone was together I saluted the guys goodbye and said, "Welp. I'm going to the beach now. See ya!"

"Wait. You're going to the beach? It's 2 in the morning."

"Yep! We're going to Clearwater right now!"

"You're crazy."

"Maybe. Have a good night, gentlemen".

With that, we piled in my car and drove. It took us almost two hours to get to Clearwater. We did, however, take a pit stop at a 24-hour Starbucks that we found on the way. The baristas there told us that we were just as crazy as the boys at McDonald's had told us, but we were not to be stopped. It was around 4 in the morning when we piled up our shoes on the beach and our toes hit the sand. The next two hours plays through my mind like some sort of nostalgic video montage. We were throwing sand at each other, running just at the edge of the water, laughing at how cold the waves were when they hit our feet. We gathered around and watched a crab walk across the sand, and Jamie even picked up Legs and carried her out into the water. We took so many pictures, and eventually we just laid down in the sand and took selfies, trying to fit all four heads in one picture. It was amazing.

Veronica and Legs walked up to a nearby hotel to go to the bathroom, leaving me alone with Jamie on the beach. We sat by the water and talked for a few minutes until he leaned in and kissed me. To which I thought to myself, why not? Kissing an ICP at 5 in the morning on a beautiful, empty beach didn't seem like such a bad idea at all.

We left the beach at around 6. We still had a two-hour drive ahead of us, and while Jamie and Veronica had already announced that they planned on sleeping the whole way home, Legs promised that she would help keep me awake. Sure enough, not 15 minutes into the drive home I looked in my rear view mirror and saw Veronica and Jamie cuddling in my back seat, passed out. It was too adorable. Legs stayed awake for the first hour, but at one point I looked over and found her to be asleep, too. So much for keeping me awake. There were beautiful colors in the sunrise Florida sky, the air was much warmer than Colorado's would have been on an early February morning, and the all-too familiar Blink-182 soundtrack was playing through my speakers. I was comfortable, but unfortunately, too comfortable. It wasn't until the loud sounds produced by the car driving over the ridges on the side of the road woke everyone up with a scream that I realized I had fallen asleep.

Actually, all four of us in the car woke up yelling "Good Morning!" in perfect unison. I don't know how, but the other three were so distracted with how hilarious our simultaneous greeting was that nobody noticed how terrified and upset I was that I had fallen asleep. They just kept laughing, and I pretended to laugh along with them. One thing was for sure—we were all awake now, and we all stayed awake until we got home. Veronica went to sleep as soon as we walked into our apartment, but Legs and I still had breakfast reservations at 'Ohana and it was too late to cancel without getting my credit card charged. Legs kept telling me how much she wanted to eat there, and so after she had a hard week at work, I made the reservations on my lunch break and sent her a screenshot of the confirmation. I think it meant a lot to her. We had a great time at 'Ohana, and the food was absolutely amazing. (What could be better than Mickey Waffles in the morning, right?). But we were falling asleep at the breakfast table.

That whole night evolved from sporadic decisions, and it was one of the best weekends of my entire program. Despite almost killing my friends, and finding sand in my car and in my shoes for weeks after, I didn't regret a bit of it. It was my first real adventure!

Chapter Five

As another week passed, work was getting easier...relatively speaking. Since some of the original Housekeeping CPs from the start of the program were already self-terming (leaving the program voluntarily), we took on two more CPs in our location, Alexis and Ashley. Alexis thought that Keven didn't like her because he was always sending her back to rooms she had already cleaned to fix things. Wyatt and I had become a stronger team and together we would finish by 3:45 every day and then go help Ashley and Alexis finish their rooms. Wyatt was getting irritated because they were falling behind so much, but I didn't mind. I liked to help; it made me feel better. The truth was that I was starting to get upset about how much Wyatt was helping me with my rooms, regardless of how much he said it didn't bother him. I just hated the feeling that I was so dependent on him. What was worse was that he never let me do anything to repay him. He wouldn't even let me do as much as hold the door open for him, or pay for my own food when we made trips to McDonald's after work, but I guess that's just the kind of person he was.

One of the rules about housekeeping is that for anyone who has been working there for less than 90 days, no matter what time you finish your board you aren't allowed to clock out until 4:30pm. This meant that every day that Wyatt and I finished early, we were usually sitting in Michael and Keven's office waiting to be able to leave. Some days, though, I really liked it. It gave me a chance to get to know my leaders. I got to learn about Keven's family, and how he grew into leadership after starting out as just a houseperson at Coronado Springs. We talked a lot with Michael about things related to the College Program; it was fun to hear about how the program had changed since he was in it. Michael also told us that he was in entertainment at one point, as a character performer, and one day he took a piece of paper and drew the signatures for all the characters that he used to be "friends with" and gave it to me. I still have it hanging on my wall.

It was during one of these talks while we were waiting to clock out that Michael asked how long we were staying. Both Wyatt and I answered at the same time, but the horror struck me when his answer was not the same as mine.

"I'm sorry what did you just say?" I asked Wyatt.

"May."

"Your program ends in MAY?"

"Yes..."

"No! You can't leave before I do! I can't do this without you!"

I tried to make it look like I was joking as much as I could, but on the inside I was shattered. I really believed that I couldn't do house-keeping without him. He had helped me with my rooms so much that there was no way I would be able to finish my boards on time if he wasn't there. I went home in a panic, and finally buckled and called Health Services again to check on the status of my request. The woman on the phone told me that my request had been approved and my medical restriction would now be listed as "Not allowed to work with or be exposed to cleaning chemicals". She told me that the next step was to wait for process management to let my leader know, and if my leaders reported back saying that they could not accommodate for me, then they would discuss recasting me.

The next day at work, they sent one of the trainers, Carmen, to follow us around to see how we were doing on our rooms. She kept coming in and pulling me back to other rooms that I had already cleaned to point out things that I had missed. I was getting frustrated because she was pulling me back for seemingly insignificant things like the toilet paper not being folded into a triangle in a stay-over room. After a few rooms that had details just as small as that one missing, I was getting angry. I had rooms to clean and a board to finish and I didn't have time to keep going back to rooms over things that didn't matter. She was pointing out stuff that none of the managers had ever pointed out to me before. I was not in the mood to deal with it. The day got worse when she would leave for a while, go look at Wyatt's rooms, and then come back in asking questions like, "Why don't you use your bed wedge? Wyatt uses his bed wedge. Why don't you clean your mirrors like Wyatt? Why don't you scrub the tub like Wyatt?" I was going to scream if I heard Wyatt's name one more time.

At one point, she came into the room that I was cleaning, watched me for a few seconds, and then finally said, "I get the feeling that you think you're bad at this. Do you think you're bad at cleaning rooms?"

I snapped. "No! I don't think I'm bad at all! A little slower, maybe, but my QA scores came back at a 94% this week, so I know that I'm not bad!"

She just looked at me, disapprovingly, and said, "Well, I think you need to be retrained. I'm going to tell the manager that you need to be sent back to training."

As soon as she left I sat down and started to cry, I was angry and upset. I had been working so hard at trying to be better at housekeeping, and because of my QA score I thought I was doing well. I texted Wyatt and told him what Carmen had said. He responded, "I'm so sorry," but what could he do? When the day was over and I went to turn in my key at the manager's office, I asked Keven if Health Services had told him anything yet. He just shook his head.

I had the next two days off work, and when I returned it was with a better mental attitude than when I had left. That was until Keven was done passing out boards and I didn't get one. He informed me that I was being sent back to training, this time with Carmen, who was standing there with a smug look on her face. Wyatt was standing next to me, and he had become a good enough friend that he could tell when I was upset even if others couldn't. "I'm going to the Pargo... are you coming with me?" he asked. I just sighed. "Yep". I followed him out, leaving Carmen behind as she talked to one of her housekeeper friends. Wyatt acted as his normal charming self on the ride over, trying to cheer me up, and when we got to the Mighty Ducks building he assured me that he would check up on me and would see me at lunch.

Training with Carmen was starting to go better than expected. How she taught me to make beds was a lot easier than the way I had been making them for the past month. The reason was that she was using her bed wedge. When they taught us at Disney University how to make beds using the wedge, I hated it; the wedge was constantly falling out and causing more of an issue than it was worth. So, when I started at All-Star, I went in with the mentality that I was never going to use one. The way that Carmen explained how to make the beds using the wedge made more sense, and as it turns out, they use the old bed wedges at the university (that do, in fact, fall out more often than not), but the wedges they use at the resorts were redesigned and worked the way they were supposed to. (Why they don't use the redesigned wedges at the university, I don't know.)

The only thing about training with Carmen was that she used a lot more chemicals than I did, and she used a lot of bleach (which I never used in my rooms). For safety reasons, we are not allowed to leave the door to the rooms open, and after an hour or so I was sitting outside the room gasping for air. I went to the linen closet and got myself a mask, but it didn't help, and after 20 minutes I was back outside gasping for air just as Michael and Keven were coming to check up on us. When they asked if I was okay, I explained that Carmen used more chemicals than I could handle, and I asked them again if they had heard anything from Health Services. Keven said, "No, Process Management will let me know if it's been approved or not, but I haven't heard anything."

"It's been approved," I told him, "they told me a few days ago that they approved it and sent it to Process Management."

"If that's the case, it should be listed on the Hub (Disney's intranet for cast members); give me a minute, I'll go look."

Keven and Michael left and parted ways, but Keven came back a few minutes later and told me, "Yep, so come on, let's go. Your medical restriction says that you're not allowed to work with or be exposed to cleaning chemicals, so we can't have you cleaning rooms. I called Process Management, and they're not sure whether they're going to terminate your program."

I stopped in my tracks "Woah. No. Health Services never said anything to me about being terminated. I was told I would be recast if my restriction got approved."

"Maybe they will. I'm not sure yet. We have to wait for Process Management to fill us in. Until then, I'm going to find a project for you to work on."

Keven started radio calling some of the other leaders around the resort trying to find a project that I could work on. For a while nobody was calling back, so he told me, "Well, since I know that this is your major and we can't just sit around and wait, I'm thinking I can show you some of the leadership role. Let's go over how room inspections work and then I'll show you the computer system we use."

I was thrilled. Keven told me that they normally only let the CPs shadow the leaders at the end of their programs, but since I was most likely going to be transferred to a new role, he wanted me to be able to see some of this while I had the chance. I couldn't be more thankful that he was willing to do that for me, but that's the difference between leaders and managers. Leaders want to help their cast grow and learn instead of just getting the job done. Keven taught me that; he taught me a lot that day.

For the rest of that day I went to the *Fantasia*-themed buildings, delivering phone books to rooms with four other people who were on modified duty. Michael told me at the end of the day to report to work as usual in the morning, and they would give me another project to do. I did this for two weeks. I would come to work in the morning, watch all of the housekeeper's boards get passed out, sit at the table with all the leaders and talk to them, wait for Process Management to come and give me a project to do, have lunch with Wyatt, finish my project. Rinse and repeat. The projects were almost always delivering phone books between rooms, but it went across property. Some days I would be in Music, other days Sports, and other days Movies. I was meeting the leaders and housekeepers from each of those sites. It was interesting how each building had its own personality. I would often overhear people say things like, "The Fantasia housekeepers are this way, or the Country Music housekeepers are that way." It was strange. I never experienced it until I was floating between buildings and becoming aware of the group dynamics. Some groups were more welcoming than others. For instance, one day a nice guy named James drove me to the Country Music building.
"Have you ever been to Country Music before?"
"No, sir."
"Oh, well. I'll give you a tour. 3rd floor. 2nd floor. 1st floor. Bam."
I laughed. "Thank you, James." He was a comical guy, and he checked up on me throughout the day. I left my coffee mug on a shelf in the Housekeeping closet room, and was told that nobody would bother it. When I got moved to Rock and Roll later in the day, I went to get my bag and my coffee mug, and of course my mug had been stolen. James was outraged, and he personally went to every housekeeper's cart until he found who had taken it, and then gave it back to me. I was flattered that he went through the trouble, but offended that my mug had been stolen in the first place. We're adults here. Although I would soon learn otherwise, it was still in my head that "this is Disney, everyone is supposed to be magical here". But more on that later.

My modified duty continued, and in some ways it worked out well for me. In the mornings I had more time to talk with the leaders and get to know them. Michael and I got along well and always had a lot to talk about in the morning, I found out that his life's dream was to be a face character, like Prince Phillip, while Keven just really liked YouTube videos and his favorite thing to say was, "Ain't nobody got time for that." Marlene, one of my favorite leaders, told me that she moved here from Puerto Rico to do a professional internship, and that was her first time in America or at a Disney theme park. She came here by herself not knowing anyone else, which was scary, but she made it because now she's one of the best leaders at All-Star.

Many people hear about women working together and immediately think of cattiness, gossip, and drama. I believe that women can be the biggest supporters of one another other. Everywhere I go, I try to find an older woman to partner with, learn from, and grow with. Since Marlene was the only female leader, I made it a point to build a relationship with her—and I am so thankful I did.

To illustrate, the people who designed these..beautiful...costumes for All-Star Housekeeping were clearly male. The costume included a bright highlighter green top, with *white* pants. Housekeeping is primarily a woman's role at Disney, and they're making us wear white pants. You can do the math. Sure enough, the nightmare about the costume came true. I went to the bathroom between rooms one day and realized what time of the month it was and I was horrified. I took my dark blue All-Star Jacket and tied it around my waist and asked everyone where I could find Marlene. "Well, I'm not sure, but is it something I can help you with?" was the common response, and my answer was always, "No. I need Marlene and Marlene only."

I finally found her in the lunch room and begged her for help. She arranged for me to be driven back to base so I could get a new costume and she gave me extra supplies as well. It was one of the most embarrassing days, and I'm so glad she was there. Ladies, get to know your female leaders. Support each other. It'll come in handy.

After being on modified duty for two-and-a-half weeks, I got a call from Health Services. The woman on the phone asked why I had submitted a restriction request. I told her that I had tried hard with housekeeping, but was worried about the effects of the chemicals on my asthma, especially with the summer months coming up and high humidity, which would make the situation worse. I told her that the last thing I wanted was to go home—this program and the Disney company meant a lot to me, and I wasn't ready to leave. She seemed to understand and told me to keep going to work and doing projects until she called me again. She had to contact my current leaders, Process Management, and my potential new leader before she could give me a definitive answer.

The next few days were Keven's days off, and Michael was taking me under his wing. Process Management wasn't even trying to give me more projects, and so Michael would just tell me that I was working with him that day and to meet him at his office at 9:00am. When I got there, he would give me a tracking sheet that showed every room in the Mighty Ducks buildings, which housekeepers were in which section, and which rooms were checkouts. My job was to go to the rooms that were check outs and take out all of the linen and trash before the housekeeper arrived. Some of the housekeepers didn't want my help, so I would just cross off their section on my sheet; some housekeepers only wanted me to do certain rooms; and some housekeepers were mostly done with their check outs by time I got there (check-out rooms are always cleaned first). Occasionally, Michael would find me and ask me to go to another section to assist a housekeeper. He did this multiple times, and I was constantly running back and forth between buildings and helping as many housekeepers as possible.

At the end of the first day, Michael gave me my first "4 Keys Fanatic" card for helping so many housekeepers with their check outs. Getting a 4 Keys card was one of my biggest goals for the program, and it meant a lot to get one from Michael. I took it home and pinned it on the cork board on my wall for future motivation.

Every day Michael and I had a routine: he would give me the tracking sheet, I would go off and work, and as needed he would find me and send me to another section. Then, at 2:00pm, we would meet back at his office and reassess the check-out situation. On the third day, after our 2:00 meeting, I had left to help Carmen strip her rooms when Health Services called and told me that I was going to be switched to Main Entrance Operations at the Magic Kingdom. Carmen probably thought that I was an idiot because I was so excited and jumping up and down while on the phone. Mostly, though, I was relieved that I was not getting termed. The woman on the phone told me that she would notify my future leaders that I had accepted the new role, and that I would get a call from them soon about when and where to report. After work, I ran into Michael's office and told him. He seemed happy, but also disappointed.

The next day Michael was off, so I was sent to do projects in one of the Dalmatians buildings. During work I got the email for my new training schedule. I started on Saturday, which meant that this was my last day at the All-Star. I told Wyatt, who didn't really care, but Keven was excited for me. I asked Wyatt what I could do to pay him back for all of his help with housekeeping. I offered to pay for him and his girlfriend to go to the movies or to buy him dinner or something, but all he wanted was a blue princess cupcake from the Main Street Confectionery. So the next day Ashley (one of the other CP housekeepers) and I went to the Magic Kingdom to meet characters and to get Wyatt his cupcake. We took it back to the All-Star and waited in Michael's office for Wyatt to be done with his rooms. Michael wasn't in his office, so we just sat down. When he came in and saw us, he started laughing and we told him about how we met Mickey Mouse and Gaston earlier that day.

He glanced down at me and said, "So I heard you had your last day already?"

"Yes, sir."

"Well, that's good. Actually, that's not good, but whatever."

I tried to laugh it off with an "aw, Michael!" but he wouldn't even look at me. A few minutes later I told him that we should be Facebook friends and keep in touch, which he agreed to do, yet he still wasn't making much conversation with me. So, as soon as Wyatt came in, we left.

And this closes my short but memorable time at the ll-Star resorts.

Chapter Six

After my medical restriction got approved, I was recast to Main Street Operations. This meant that I was working in the Town Square Theater, giving information to guests about the park and the theater, as well as running the meet-and-greet line for Mickey Mouse. I was also working the Sorcerers of the Magic Kingdom game (an interactive scavenger hunt that included spell cards, magic portals, and fighting nine villains throughout the Magic Kingdom). I often joked that SoMK was like Disney Pokemon, but in reality it was a lot of fun, and some guests get pretty obsessed with it.

My first day of training was a class called "Once Upon a Time... Is Now!" The name was taken from a quote of Walt's when he was describing the Magic Kingdom, and the class was a 4-hour walking tour of the park. We learned about its obscure details and hidden secrets. For instance, in Liberty Square, the Liberty Bell on display there was poured out of the same mold as the actual Liberty Bell, making the two "sisters". After our Liberty Bell was made, the mold broke, so the only two bells that exist are ours and the original. Next to the bell we have the Liberty Tree, with 13 lanterns hanging from it. Each lantern represents one of the original 13 colonies, and if you look closely, the lanterns have different designs to represent its colony. We also learned that at 5pm, every day, the American flag is taken down in a grand ceremony, in accordance with tradition, but the smaller American flags that line the rooftops of Main Street remain up overnight. While that might sound strange, it's because those smaller flags are fake— missing a star or stripe, *something*—and so it's not required to take them down at the end of the day.

We discussed again the 4 Keys of Safety, Courtesy, Show, and Efficiency. While we were discussing Show, we approached the attraction that perhaps has the best example of show in the park: the Haunted Mansion. Eerie music plays from somewhere within the mansion, there's a cemetery outside, the roses always grow blood red, the Cast

Members don't smile, and occasionally they stand near the queue line with their ghost dog on a leash. Our tour guide asked us, through the whisper unit plugged into our ears which let the guide communicate with us and not have guests overhear him, "Would you guys like to go ride the Haunted Mansion?". The effort to remain professional was immense. I was actually getting paid to ride the Haunted Mansion.

The next day we took the "For Our Guests" class, which was little more than a Main Street orientation. We walked in and out of every gift shop and learned the history of the Main Street windows, Walt's apartment with the light that will never turn off, and the "Casting Agency" door (a tribute from Walt to every cast member that ever was, is, and will be). I checked out my new costume—navy blue pants, a white button-up, a navy blue vest, a red bow tie, for when it gets "cold", a navy blue blazer. It's adorable, much better that the bright green-and-white nonsense that was my Housekeeping costume. Our facilitator, Pattie, took us to the Liberty Bridge so we could watch the Fantasy of Festival parade, which had premiered the day before. The Mad Hatter ran up to Nicole, one of the cast members in our group, saying "You're earning your ears? But you already have ears! So I guess you've earned them!" and then danced away. Tears filled my eyes when Tiana blew me a kiss and Elsa threw her snow in the air. I felt like I was starting my program over, and this is how it *should* have started.

The next day was my official "first day of training", along with three male cast members. We reported to Carlos, who went over every position with us, and then had us practice them. Carlos seemed like a great buy, but I noticed that he was a little bitter. He was upset with how cast members were being treated. I didn't think it wise to ask him about it, so I tried not to notice. After having worked at the Marriott, I knew that business politics was something to avoid. The only thing that really stuck with me during one of his rants was this observation: "You'll start to notice as you're walking back stage, there's nothing but angry cast members. Sure we're all magical on stage but back here, almost nobody smiles anymore."

As the week went on and I began walking through the Magic Kingdom tunnels (Utilidors) on the way to and from Main Street, I noticed that Carlos was right. I mostly walked past the people who worked in the Confectionery and the Plaza Ice Cream Parlor, since we shared the same break room, and just as Carlos had said, nobody smiled; in fact, they looked pretty angry. Even on the days that I would venture over to the cast member cafeteria, whimsically called the Mouseketeria (these days were few and far between, since it was a mile away from the Town Square Theater), I notice that even the princesses and other characters seemed sad or angry. Even the Dapper Dans rarely smiled backstage.

I began to wonder what it was really like to work for the mouse.

The rest of training went smoothly. In general, both the theater and SoMK were easy to learn. On my second day of actual training, I was assigned to work with Carlos again. He spent a couple of hours teaching me the SoMK game. He showed me the opening position, which requires walking to each of the different lands and testing out a couple of the portals. While we were in Adventureland he mentioned the Pirate Adventure scavenger hunt game, and suggested that we play to "learn about what else the park offers". The game was a lot of fun; it makes things "come alive" throughout Adventureland, such as cannons going off, Tiki men talking, and other magical things.

After playing the game for a while, Carlos trained me on the computer system for SoMK (how to issue spell cards, how to start people on a new game, etc). We spent an hour on this task and then we took our break. During the break, he had me fill out the assessment tests for the theater and SoMK, congratulated me on passing, and then bought me a cupcake from the Yum Yum Cupcake truck that was parked back stage for the day. It was one of the easiest training sessions I have ever had, especially when compared to my week of tear-filled training in Housekeeping.

At the end of the day, I tore off my red "Earning My Ears" ribbon for the second time and went home to my semi-empty apartment. Jessica was at Adam's, the twins were sleeping, Veronica was at Vista, and Legs was on the phone, watching a movie with her long-distance boyfriend. I curled up on the couch and watched Netflix until I fell asleep, exhausted but completely content with the new direction that my program was taking.

Chapter Seven

It was right about this time that my family (consisting of Mom, younger brother, an aunt, and a cousin) decided to visit. It was stressful planning their trip because we had started preparations for it while I was still working at All-Star, not knowing whether I was going to be termed before they arrived. Luckily I made it, and so did they.

Their week here was...stressful. My cousin is young and impatient with lines. We would set up FastPass times, but when our slots came around she was no longer interested in that attraction. My little brother is autistic and doesn't care much for crowds. Nobody in my family really does, come to think of it.

Our first day at Magic Kingdom was long, very long. My family had enjoyed their time at Downtown Disney, which had just started its transformation into Disney Springs, and the road construction was just beginning to become unbearable. By day three, my aunt and cousin wouldn't even go to Hollywood Studios with us. They opted to for the hotel pool, so my mom and my brother and I went on our own. They had a wonderful time, and that's when I learned the greatest thing about my brother: because he is autistic, he has to know how everything works, and I mean *everything*. The longer he was at Disney, the more he was getting frustrated with not being able to learn how things worked and was getting tired of hearing "Disney magic" as an answer. For instance, throughout the entire day at Magic Kingdom, this observant child never saw the line in the sky coming out of the castle. So when Tinker Bell flew that night, he just about lost his mind.

"HOW IS SHE DOING THAT!? THAT'S AMAZING!"

"Dude. She's a fairy. She has wings. Duh."

"Yeah, okay, Cami. But how is she FLYING?"

"Because she's a FAIRY."

We had conversations like this the whole weekend. When we saw the Voyage of the Little Mermaid at Hollywood Studios, my brother didn't see that Ariel already had the blue dress on in the end scene. In his head, all he knows is that one second she's wearing a seashell bra and a tail, and the next she's in a blue dress. He still doesn't know how it happened; I just keep telling him that it was magic. He'll figure it out eventually.

The best, however, was when we were watching Fantasmic! Now, Fantasmic! is my favorite show—I swear it's the only thing that stopped me from self-terming during Housekeeping. I wasn't going to let my family get away without watching it. When it was over, my mom kept saying how much she loved it, but my brother was huffing and puffing about how much he hated Disney.

"What's wrong, bro? You didn't like it?"

"No, it was wonderful. I just...don't...understand."

"What don't you understand?"

"How they lit the water on fire! You can't just do that! It's WATER; it doesn't BURN!"

"Dude, it's Disney mag—"

"Say it's Disney magic one more time, Cami, I dare you."

So my mom and I offered our ideas to him about how the effect was done, but he couldn't wrap his head around a single one. "I'm just going to have to talk to my science teacher about this. I swear nothing in this place makes sense." (In case you were wondering, I found out the real secret behind it. There's a bunker filled with natural gas that sits behind the audience. The gas flows through valves to stainless steel tubing that has holes punched in it, so as the gas floats out of the holes to the surface of the water, the pyro platforms have big spark plugs that cause the fire to light, and spread. Disney Magic!)

It was great having my family in town, as stressful as it was, but it still wasn't hitting me how much I was missing home. In my mind I was still anti- Colorado and determined to stay in Florida forever. It broke my heart a little when we were on the ferry boat leaving Magic Kingdom and my family told me they were glad to be going home and planned never to return. I felt awful after they left, not really sure that they liked anything at all, except for my mom's favorite, the Electrical Parade, which is similar to the one we watched in Disneyland when I was a kid. I never understood why it was different for me than it was for the twins and their family. For them, every time their mom came into town and left again, they missed her and home more and more, whereas I felt like I was distancing myself, which is what I thought I wanted. I guess I was too overcome by Disney magic to notice how much I really did miss and need my family.

About a month later, I was sitting in my apartment when I got a call from my best friend back home, Megan, who told me that she'd been saving up money to come and see me. She was going to make it a surprise, but then decided she should give me a heads-up so that I could get time off work. She'd be here in a few weeks.

It was the best news I'd had in a while. I started planning out our week together, making dining reservations and checking out the different resorts (in the end, I chose to book a room at Caribbean Beach). I picked up as many shifts as I could to earn money for while she was here, and everything worked perfectly. On the day of her arrival, by Magical Express from the airport, I remember sitting outside of the Caribbean Beach waiting for almost an hour for her bus to arrive. Every time a Magical Express bus pulled in, my head would perk up like a dog's when there's a knock on the door, but it was never her. Finally, I saw her big blue eyes poking through one of the windows of the giant bus and I screamed with excitement. Megan and I have been best friends for 15 years, and I couldn't wait to show her my world.

During check-in, Megan and I were trying to pay attention to everything that the girl was telling us, but she made the mistake of giving us both glitter-coated star wands. Let me tell you something about these wands: anything that it touches turns to glitter. Naturally, as soon as I had it in my hand, I smacked Megan in the chest with it, watching a puff of glitter radiate off of the wand and surround her. Then, as we were getting driving directions and park information from the cast member, we were attacking each other with the wands, trying our hardest to look like we were paying attention. After we were in our room for a while, I noticed that the bed was covered in glitter. When I was in Housekeeping, I would so often walk into rooms that were covered in glitter (and I mean covered, buried, smothered in layers and layers of sparkle). I used to have to always change sheets because the glitter makes them seem dingy, and I remember thinking, 'How does somebody get this much glitter IN EVERY CORNER OF THEIR BED?' and now, looking down at the sparkle-saturated sheets, I finally understood why and laughed.

The entire week with Megan was perfect. We didn't have to wait in line for anything, we had amazing character interactions, and we actually got to meet almost every character in the parks. We scored amazing seats for shows and parades. We ate dinner at Tony's Town Square restaurant one night, which is as good as I imagined it would be. (When you work in Town Square Theater, you're forced to endure the delicious smells of Tony's, day in and day out.) We also ate at 1900 Park Fare at the Grand Floridian, with appearances by Cinderella, Prince Charming, and the Tremaines. It's still my favorite dining experience.

The best part of the week was when Megan and I made a magical moment together. We had two re-admit paper FastPasses (sometimes they hand these out if you're on a ride while it breaks down or something similar). The ones we had could get you anywhere in the park, including characters appearances, and we hadn't really planned on where to use them yet. While we were waiting in line to meet Tinker Bell, we ended up talking to this little girl who was telling us all about her day and the fairies and how her favorite princess was Ariel and she really wanted to meet her. The mom told us that she hadn't been able to get FastPasses for Ariel, despite her best efforts. I asked her about Anna and Elsa, and she said she wasn't even going to try, nor was she going to bring it up around the little one.

"Believe me," the mom told us, "she loves Elsa and Anna, obsessed, actually. There's no way I could even try to make that one work, though."

Megan and I looked at each other knowingly, and I gave our FastPasses to the little girl's mom, her she could use them to see Ariel. Megan interrupted me, saying "Or you can use them to meet Anna and Elsa." The mother's face dropped.

"We can use these? To get in the FastPass line? For Anna and Elsa? Are you serious?"

I smiled at her and told her that yes, she could, and she started to cry. "Thank you so much, you have no idea how amazing this is."

She got down on her knees and told her daughter about how we had given her FastPasses to go see Elsa and Anna. The little girl jumped with excitement and gave both Megan and I hugs. After thanking us, she looked at her mom and said, "Don't cry, Mom. It's okay." Which only made her mom cry more, naturally.

We got to watch the little girl meet Tinker Bell, her mom tearing up the entire time telling us, "It's still so real for her, you know? It's amazing."

They waved goodbye to us as they left Pixie Hollow to resume their vacation. Megan couldn't have been more excited about what we had done. I told her that this was what being a cast member was like—getting to make magical moments every single day.

Later the day, Megan and I had just finished watching the Hall of Presidents show and were sitting on the rocking chairs by the exit, taking a few minutes to relax. After a minute or so, here came the mom and her daughter from the Tinker Bell line, with their entire family in tow.

"That's them! Those are the girls who gave us tickets to see Anna and Elsa!"

The girl ran straight to me and gave me a huge hug, thanking me again. "You're welcome, sweetheart," I told her. Her dad came over and shook our hands, thanking us and telling us how much it meant to them that she would get to see Anna and Elsa this trip, after all. I smiled and told them how happy I was for them. I said, "I work here. I get to see these characters every day, but this is your vacation. It deserves to be as magical as it can possibly be."

I guess Megan got a little teary-eyed that night during Wishes thinking about that family. She was able to experience what it feels like to be a cast member. I'm glad I could share that with her.

Chapter Eight

During one of my first few weeks on Main Street, I met Bobby and Mikey in the theater pit as I was ending my shift. (The pit is an area underneath the theater where we clock in and out and take our breaks sometimes; Mickey also passes through there to get to his dressing room.) I began talking with them as well as with another girl, Amanda. Somehow, the conversation escalated into a screaming match between myself and Bobby over Princess Aurora and why she may or may not be a useless princess. (For the record, she's the *best* princess; don't let anyone ever say otherwise). If I remember correctly, the exact quote from Bobby was, "And what princess are you, Cami? The one who's budget got slashed because the story line sucked and nobody cared about her so they never finished the movie?"

Bobby and Mikey invited me to come hang around Magic Kingdom with them for a couple of hours, until Mikey had to go to work. I thought Bobby was strange; he joked around more often than not, which made conversation hard to sustain, and he seemed really pleased with himself.

The next week, I came down into the pit again after my shift to clock out, and there he was sitting in the same spot as he had been when I first saw him.

"Oh, yes!" he said when he saw me, and jumped up to give me a hug. We spent some time together around Magic Kingdom and decided to go to Be Our Guest for lunch the next week.

My first assignment was at the Christmas Shoppe, which is all the way over in Liberty Square. Bobby offered to walk me to the Christmas Shoppe, insisting that we "stroll up Main Street" on the way and he complimented my eyes as we walked. I was starting to see the real charm in Bobby...but the feeling didn't last. When we went to Be Our Guest for lunch, we had to wait in line for almost two hours—those two hours consisted of what he called "playing games" and included a lot of making fun of me and putting me down. By the end of the day I had tear-filled eyes and I was officially over Bobby.

I saw him again the next week when I clocked in and my assignment was to give him his break.

"Weren't you just so thrilled to see that you were working with me today?" he gloated as I handed him his break slip.

"Sure, Bobby. Real thrilled."

"Oh, I see you've turned against me."

As he strutted away to take his break, one of the full timers, Knicola, told me that the secret to making Bobby "behave himself" was to just look at him and not say anything—give him no attention. So when Bobby came back with the "What's wrong?" I kept quiet. Five minutes later, there was the "Why do you hate me?" My answer was simple: "I don't hate you, Bobby. I just don't want to spend any time with you. After we hung out last week, I went home and cried because of the things you said to me. So, thanks but no thanks, Bobby."

Bobby walked away, and I found out from someone later that he went down to the pit and started throwing things against the walls. When he returned he told me, "I'm so sorry. I miss you." And then he gave me a hug. Maybe I was getting soft in my old age, but that's what started my friendship with Bobby.

Bobby's birthday was coming up. I worked in the morning, and so did a fellow cast member, Jessica (*another* Jessica, not one of my roommates). Bobby was off a little later than we were, so Jessica and I played Sorcerers of the Magic Kingdom for a while, and when it got closer to the time that Bobby clocked out I went to Starbucks and bought him a Frappuccino. I asked the Starbucks lady to write "Happy Birthday, Bobby" on the cup. Jessica got us all buttons. Bobby got a "Happy Birthday" button, which also had "Bobby" written on it, while Jessica and I got Celebration buttons. We took Bobby to go meet princesses, and they loved him. Snow White was hanging on his arm the entire time, and even rested her head on his shoulder as she talked. Rapunzel asked him if we were his step-sisters; he looked straight at me and said, "No, they're too pretty to be step-sisters." I don't know who swooned more, me or Rapunzel.

Later in the night we were eating cupcakes in Fantasyland near the Cheshire Cafe. Things were starting to get tense, as the three of us were bickering over silly things. That's when I learned one of the most important things about Bobby: he will do anything, literally anything, to try to make you smile again. He shoved his hand into the cupcake, grabbed a handful of cake and frosting and started screaming, trying to start a food fight. Jessica stared at him like he was an idiot, but I couldn't stop laughing. The cupcake was destroyed and he was covered in pink frosting.

When he returned from washing cake off his hands, things got quiet between the three of us. Jessica finally reached over to her phone and turned on "Love Is an Open Door" from *Frozen*. Bobby started singing and kept encouraging me to sing along with him. But I don't sing in front of people, especially not in public. When I started to sing, I was embarrassed about it and kept my hands over my mouth. Bobby reached over and pulled my hands down and continued to do so until I quit being shy and actually sang along with him.

We sang "Love Is an Open Door", "A Whole New World", "So This is Love", and then finally my favorite part of the entire night: "Once Upon A Dream". Bobby knows that I'm obsessed with Sleeping Beauty (our first conversation, remember, was fighting over Aurora's importance). Bobby stood up, took me by the hand, and started waltzing me around the Cheshire Cafe area, singing in my ear.

Being friends with Bobby was something like that every day; he made every moment magical. I could write an entire book full of "Magical Moments with Bobby", but there are some moments that are just too precious to share with the rest of the world

I told Bobby earlier that day that I thought Jessica wanted to date me, and when she invited herself to spend his birthday with us I sort of knew, but Bobby wouldn't have it. "Don't start drama, Cami. Not everything is about you." So I kept quiet. But when the end of the night came, Bobby was parked in the cast member parking lot, and Jessica and I were both parked at the Ticket and Transportation Center. Sure enough, as soon as we were on the monorail, Jessica was holding my hand. I tried to play it off as a friend thing, pretending not to notice, but as we got off the monorail she told me that she did, in fact, think I was adorable, and asked me on a date. I didn't know how to respond to her. I've never been good at turning people down, but I guess I didn't need to, because she already knew. She knew I didn't like her, and she knew that I was starting to fall for Bobby. "Just know the offer is there."

She and I stayed friends, for the most part, and I continued to make even more friends on Main Street. One in particular, Becky, had a big impact on my program. Becky is a full-time cast member who's been working here for a couple years. I came to Becky about almost anything; she was my adopted mom. Her best friend, James, a coordinator for PhotoPass at Magic Kingdom, became my adopted dad. The three of us spent a lot of time as a group, taking our breaks at work together, or occasionally going to IHOP after work to talk about things going on in our lives. I loved those nights; it was like being with family. I needed that, especially on days that I felt a homesick.

And then came Greg.

Greg was a CP from California, and the first thing anyone noticed about him was how tall he was; the second thing was how nice of a person he was, to everyone around him.

I first met Greg when I was "tasking" in the theater. I noticed him standing in the middle of the rotunda, so I went to introduce myself. He asked me why we were scheduled until 12:45, when the theater closed at noon.

"Does it really take 45 minutes to close the theater?"

"No, it really takes about 5 minutes. After we're done we have the option to take an early release and go home, or go outside and wave goodnight to guests until our shift is up." I told him that my friend Travis and I like to take Mickey gloves and go on top of the train station and wave goodbye to people as they leave. (Not to mention, it is the PERFECT view for watching the Kiss Goodnight; Main Street makes a beautiful backdrop.) He asked if we could do the Mickey glove thing that night, and I was thrilled to go along with him. So, as soon as we closed the theater, Greg and I ran to the PAC room to get our Mickey gloves, took a selfie, and then went to the train station.

Events like these are some of the little things that make being a cast member magical. Guests are thrilled when they see you up there with Mickey gloves; they almost always wave back, say thank you, take pictures, blow kisses—it makes whatever stress happened earlier in the day worth it.

So that's how I met Greg, and the more time I spent with him the closer we became. Often we would carpool to work, since we generally worked similar shifts. Many nights after work we would go to his apartment and watch Disney movies with his roommate, Sean. I told him about Bobby, and Bobby about him. One night I was off and I got a text from Greg saying, "OMG! I just met Bobby! He's so nice and so handsome. We should all hang out soon!" This was soon followed by a text message from Bobby: "I just met Greg. I told him that we should all hang out, but don't worry, I was super-casual about it." That explains the start of their relationship perfectly. Bromance.

Greg, Bobby, and I spent almost every day together after that. Before work, during work, after work—we were always together. People, of course, like to talk, and I was often asked which one of them I was dating. Main Street loves to talk, but I stayed out of it. They were two of the best friends I had had for a very long time. The three of us rode the Seven Dwarfs Mine Train for the first time together during cast member previews. We rode it as many times as we could. I rode it with them 8 or 9 times before I left, and then they went back and rode it another 6 or 7 times, and apparently rode it with Phil Holmes (vice-president of the Magic Kingdom) for a round.

We were there or each other, no matter what, and we helped each other through heartbreaks. As it turned out, the girl that Bobby was involved with, Kayla, went to the same school in California as Greg. And Greg had an ex back home who had broken his heart. I was still fixed on Harrison—and the boys could not have hated him any more than they did.

There were many crying and counseling sessions at the Christmas Shoppe kiosk, but there was only one true solution—drinking around the world. I was still not old enough to drink so I mediated, which Bobby quickly changed to "match-making around the world with Cami", a game in which they would try to find me a boy in every country. Greg and Bobby made it about as far as Japan until they had an emotional breakdown on the floor, holding each other crying and telling each other how handsome and wonderful the other one was and how much better they deserved. They cried again in America, and then in Italy it was my turn and they sat me on a bench and kissed my cheeks and told me that I deserved better than a guy like Harrison, that Harrison was leading me on and taking me on dates, even though he had told me the week before that I wasn't worthy of a commitment because of my tattoos.

That's how we worked it all through—always dramatic, but always finding ways to cheer each other up. Greg mediated every fight that Bobby and I had (and believe me, we fought a lot) and the two of them continued on with their bromance. It was the best thing I had at the time.

Occasionally, I got to see Greg's roommate, Sean. And then one day Sean and Greg got word that I lived with twins.

"Do they want to date us?" Sean asked

"Yeah. We could totally date the twins," Greg added.

I grabbed them by their shirts and pulled them in close to me saying, "Listen to me. Stay away from the twins. Don't look at the twins. Don't talk to the twins. Don't think about the twins. They're too good for you. Don't even think about it."

They laughed it off, but a few weeks later was the big "Starlit Splash" event, when the College Program buys out Typhoon Lagoon overnight for CPs. We got free T-shirts, hats, sunglasses, and unlimited Mickey Bars throughout the event, and at midnight they presented us with a special fireworks show.

Greg and Sean were coming with me, and we were meeting Liz and Rachel. I told Greg and Sean not to dare hit on the twins or I would drown them, and they behaved. Except for Sean, who tried to flirt with Legs, not realizing she had a boyfriend, but that was just funny.

Almost a month later, Greg and I were getting off of work and were walking through the Utilidors to go home when we ran into Liz. Greg and I brought separate cars, so I offered to wait for Liz to get off so I could give her a ride home. As Liz and I were leaving, she asked, "That was Greg, right?"

"Yeah, that's Greg. He totally has a crush on Rachel, by the way. I told him he didn't have a chance."

"No way! Rachel totally has a crush on Greg!"

"No!"

"Yeah, she really liked him at Starlit Splash."

"This isn't happening to me."

"We have to tell her!" Liz laughed.

We got in the car and I turned up my music, drowning out the sounds of disbelief in my head.

We got home and immediately ran into the twins' room where Rachel was sitting in bed reading a book.

"Rachel, I have to tell you something," I started, Liz standing next to me laughing.

"What's up?" she asked

"Greg really likes you, but don't worry, I already told him he didn't have a prayer."

"What?!" She nearly flew out of bed.

After that, it was game over. My social life and my relationship with Greg no longer stood a chance. After that, all I heard at work was:

"How's Rachel? Did you see her last night? Did you see her this morning? Is she at work today? Does she work tomorrow? Should I call her or is it too soon? Do you think she would prefer it if I sent her a text instead of calling her? What if I interrupt something by calling her? Should I send her flowers? What kind of flowers should I send her? Hey, are you going to be home tomorrow night so i can drop off flowers? Do you think I should take her on a date? Where should I take her? Should I ask Bobby?"

All. Day. Long.

I had to hear it every single day. For weeks.

And then the two of them got serious, and Greg was at my apartment all the time. So I worked all day with Greg, and then I would come home to Greg. And it's not that I didn't love Greg, it was just *so much* Greg. Although he was my best friend, he had this amazing ability to drive me insane. I couldn't be around him for longer than five minutes without wanting to throw him out the window. Regardless, he was here, and I was genuinely happy for him and Rachel. They were the most perfect couple that I had ever seen.

One of my other friends in the theater was Chao Chen. He was the first real friend I had made who wasn't from America. Chao Chen was Chinese, he was a really sweet kid, and he taught me a couple of Chinese phrases like how to say "hello" and "goodbye" and "I love you". He even gave me my own Chinese name. I often saw him in the break room since he also worked PAC (Parade Audience Control). Most of the time he would be down there sleeping with his PAC hat hiding his face, his friend Chen sitting next to him laughing. I learned a lot from Chao Chen about how different the world is; for instance, one day we were eating lunch together and he looked at me and said, "You know if you don't stop eating so much you're never going to get married."

"Chao Chen! That's not very polite!"

"Why not?"

"You can't say that to people here. That's really rude."

"Oh. I didn't know. I was not trying to be rude. I'm sorry."

That's when I realized that it was a cultural thing for him; he wasn't trying to be rude at all. Eventually, he got transferred to the

Emporium, so I saw him even less than I already did. Sometimes I would go into the break room specifically just to see if he was there and I was always so excited when he was. One day he told me that he came in there to look for me, too, and said, "Our hearts must be connected."

A few weeks later Chao Chen's program ended and he moved back to China. I cried when I said goodbye, and when I did I said it in Chinese. Since the chances of me going to China or him coming back to America are slim to none, I doubt I'll ever see him again. That was the first time I realized how difficult that portion of this program is. You meet wonderful, beautiful people from all corners of the world, you spend so much of your time with them, but when the program's over, they're gone. It breaks your heart.

Chapter Nine

When people come to visit Disney, they're always hoping to be a part of a "magical moment"—something that makes them feel special, like they're the most important guest in the whole park. Most people don't realize that cast members get magical moments, too. My year at Disney was full of them. Sometimes my magical moments would be as small as a little princess coming to give me a hug and telling me thank you, or a little prince telling me that I was his favorite part of the day. But I had some much bigger moments, too, some that only a cast member can experience.

One night I had a leader named Marilyn come and take me on a "4 Keys Basics Walk". You're supposed to do these walks every so often with a manager and you talk about how you can use the 4 Keys in your area and point out different examples of the keys. Marilyn and I were walking through the Emporium talking about the keys when she got an alpha call over her radio. (That's an ambulance or medical emergency.) A coordinator and a leader are required to respond to alphas, so she had to go to first aid and offered to let me come with her to see what the process was like. By the time we got to first aid, however, there was now not one, but two alpha calls there. We were greeted by another of my other leaders, Frank, who was helping in one room, while Marilyn helped elsewhere. I asked Frank if there was anything that I could do. He told me that there was four little girls in the lobby who were worried about their mom and who needed to be entertained. I love little kids, so I ran out right away.

I saw them sitting on a bench talking amongst themselves; they were all very young, the oldest had to have been 9 or 10.

"Hey, ladies! I'm Cami, how are you doing?"

"Hey, Cami. We're good, How's Mom?" asked the oldest.

"She's doing alright," I told them. "How's your day been?"

Luckily, the girls weren't shy. They each took turns telling me about the favorite part of their day and how much fun they were having here, which characters they had met, and which rides they had ridden. They were so sweet and fun.

After about 15 minutes I heard a "Hey, ladies!" from behind me. It was Frank. "I just wanted to let you know that Minnie Mouse came by here, and she's really busy so she couldn't come in, but she wanted me to tell you that she says hello and she's thinking about you, and she wanted me to give you these!" He pulled out four Minnie Mouse stuffed animals and gave one to each of the kids.

Then he turned to me: "Cami. Can I talk to you for a moment?"

I followed him into the hall. "You have a valid driver's license. right?" he asked me.

"Yes?"

"Would you be comfortable driving a 15-passenger van?"

"Um, yeah, sure—what's up?"

"Their mom has pretty bad crowd anxiety and we need to get her to their car at the TTC without putting her on a monorail or ferry boat, and we can't get hold of a driver. So I figured we'd ask you, since you've already made a connection with the family."

"Oh, sure, no problem. I'd love to." (I could not have been more nervous.)

"Great. Go ahead and play with the girls some more, and I'll come let you guys know when we're ready."

I turned around and went back to the lobby. The youngest girl asked me, "Cami, do you know how many stuffies we have? Like, 200, and now that we have these, it's like 300."

I laughed and said, "Listen, girls, real talk, I am 20 years old and I have at least 12 stuffies in my bed."

The younger three girls laughed so hard they were doubled over hugging their Minnies; they must have thought it was the funniest thing they had ever heard. But the oldest didn't laugh. She sagged her head and said, "I wish I could do that. My mom only lets us have three stuffies in our bed with us."

I didn't know what to say, so I just told her that one day she would grow up, and then she could work at Disney World and have as many stuffies in her bed as she wanted. It must have worked because it made her laugh.

The girls then asked me about how I liked working here, if I thought my costume was too hot, and how I kept from passing out in the summer. They wanted to know if the princesses got lonely living in that big castle by themselves. Our conversation got interrupted by Frank and their dad walking in, with their mom in the wheelchair. The older three yelled "Mom!" and ran to her, but the youngest ran to me instead and whispered in my ear, "Can I tell my mom your story?"

"Which story?" I asked her

"About the stuffies!" she said, hitting my leg in excitement.

I buried my face in my hands laughing, and thought: 'Oh, no, what have I done?' But I said, "Sure, sweetheart, go ahead."

"MOM!!" she yelled, pointing at me, "Cami is 20 years old and she gets 12 stuffies in her bed!!!"

I looked at the mom with an apologetic look, but she immediately grabbed my arm, tears pouring down her cheeks, and said, "Thank you." I smiled back at her and her daughters hugged her and asked why she was crying. "I was just worried about you, of course," she told them.

Frank introduced me to their dad and told him that I was going to be driving them back to their car.

"We already know Cami," the dad said

"We do?" I ask

"Well, sure, you taught us how to play Sorcerers of the Magic Kingdom this morning. It's good to see you again."

I laughed it off, but all I could think in my mind was, "Amazing. Disney magic."

We got them safely to their car safe and the whole family gave me a big hug goodbye. I'll never forget them. I've forever added the word "stuffie" to my personal dictionary, and every time I get a new one I think of those little girls and how proud they would be that I now have 21 stuffies in my bed.

That was the night I learned about leaders who do compassionate care work for guests. It's similar to what I had just done—going above and beyond for our guests who get injured here. Some leaders even make hospital visits. I made it a personal goal of mine to learn more, and to make it a career goal for the future. I never would have even known that compassionate care work existed if it weren't for that alpha call. It made me fall in love with the company even more.

There was one day that I was working Sorcerers of the Magic Kingdom at the Christmas Shoppe, and I trained a family how to play. There were three kids: two girls and a boy. I feel bad for saying it, but

I only remember one of their names, and that was Brooke. Brooke was excited about the game, and after I was done training her and her family, I was giving her parents advice as to where to watch the fireworks and the parades. I was interrupted at one point by little Brooke hugging my side, looking up at me and saying, "You're my new best friend." I just smiled and hugged her back, saying, "You're my new best friend, too!" I talked with her family some more and Brooke asked me to sign her autograph book. It was one that had the page on one side and a place to put a photo on the other, so naturally we had to take a picture together as well. I took pictures and signed the autograph books of her siblings as well. (I always signed as "Princess Cami" with pixie dust, just for fun.)

The next day I had off, and when I returned to work the day after Marilyn asked me to come to her office, where I received my first reprimand. I was under the impression, for whatever reason, that we had a 3-minute grace period when we were clocking in, so it didn't matter if we were 30 seconds late. I was wrong about that, and Marilyn corrected me. I guess I should have asked about it sooner. Regardless, I was bummed out about the reprimand and worried that it might affect my chance to extend my program. I sulked back to the theater with my head down when someone came up and told me that there was a cast member looking for me in the firehouse. I walked over and found who was looking for me and asked what the problem was.

"I have something for you," she said, and handed me a poorly folded paper from her pocket that read "To Cami From Brooke" on the front.

"To Cami from Brooke Mullner. Did you see the fireworks? It was nice to meet you. This is to my new best friend. You are nice. Thank you for teaching me."

Tears filled my eyes. I folded the note and put it in my pocket and thanked the cast member who gave it to me. At the end of the day I went home and I pinned it on my wall. I never threw it away. I've kept it to remind myself on the bad days why I do what I do here, what being a cast member really means. I had dreamt most of my life about working for this company, and it was all for moments like this. We make magical moments for our guests, and they make magical moments for us, but sometimes we get to make magical moments for each other, too.

Some nights, when Town Square Theater was slow, we would run back and say hello to the characters just before closing. It was always fun coming back to see Mickey in our costumes and listening to him tell his silly jokes. I remember one time the character attendant said to Mickey, "You have some very special guests coming to see you!" We all ran in and Mickey's only response was, "Oh. That's a good one."

Something about hanging out with Mickey Mouse at work made me feel like my life was the coolest it could ever be. One day after Bobby and I had concluded round 1 of yet another fight, the female cast member who had just finished her shift as Mickey found me crying in the pit and sat and talked with me for a minute. When I came back for my next break I found a bottle of Coca Cola in my bag along with a note from her, encouraging me to not be so blue.

Another time I was having a bad day, but I was positioned at Tinker Bell merge and the theater was slow and the character attendant went and told Tink that I was having a rough day. She invited me to come back and have "Tinker Bell time" with her. We spent a few minutes taking pictures together and she taught me how to pose like a fairy. We tried to climb the giant spoon that sits against the tree in Pixie Hollow, and at one point she accidentally hit me in the head with both of her wings. It was a little thing for her, but it meant so much to me.

Often, when I was at the firehouse either as a greeter or at check-in on a slow day, I would grab a giant bottle of bubble soap and go outside and blow bubbles, usually drawing in a giant crowd of little ones. I did this many times because I had so much fun, and it was a great way to stop kids from crying. Over time, I received several 4 Keys cards for it, and was starting to build a reputation. One night, Greg and I closed the theater and we were standing outside waving goodnight to guests when a man with a stroller containing a sleeping child stopped and said, "Hey! It's the bubble girl!"

I laughed and said, "That sounds like me."

"We were over by the firehouse the other night and you were blowing bubbles with my kid; you totally made his day. It was one of his favorite parts of his whole trip, and if he was awake right now I'm sure he would be excited to see you. Thank you so much."

I was flattered that he had recognized me. "Oh, gosh, absolutely. I had so much fun, too."

"Actually, I got quite a few pictures of you blowing bubbles. They turned out really great!" He emailed me the pictures and they were amazing. He took them from behind his kid, facing me, with all of Town Square lit up in the background. They were beautiful photos. I showed them to my managers and coordinators, thrilled to make this connection with a guest. And that's when I developed the name "The Main Street Bubble Girl". A lot of my friends, although mostly Carlos, referred to me as Bubble Girl. It was a nickname that I wore proudly. I felt like I had made a place for myself on Main Street, U.S.A.

There's a different kind of magical moment that cast members get, and it's about being behind the magic. There are some things you'll see and experience here that you never thought you would see—like the Haunted Mansion with the lights on, or my personal favorite, filming for a media event. Occasionally, TV shows will run a special in the park and need an area blocked off; cast members are sent to help, which is always cool, but my favorite was an event that took place at Epcot.

Allyson and I picked up Epcot shifts that went from three in the morning to seven in the morning, two days in a row. A crew was filming in the park and needed us to "guard" break rooms and other places where there was on-stage access to make sure no one came out during the filming. They stationed Allyson and I together in front of the security office, but since the security guards were all helping us, there really wasn't anything to guard. Allyson had brought us Dunkin Donuts coffee, and we stood and watched a helicopter fly around the park with a giant camera hanging off of it. For hours we watched it go around and around and around, and the grand finale? The sun rising over Spaceship Earth. It was one of the most beautiful things I've ever seen.

Not long after that, the company was making extensive preparations, including many media events, for the opening of a new ride, Seven Dwarfs Mine Train. One day Bobby and I were walking through Fantasyland and just happened to see Dopey ride past us on the train wearing a sweet pair of sunglasses. About a week or so later there was a large media event, and I picked up a shift to coincide with it. The difficult thing about picking up shifts outside of your area is that sometimes the instructions aren't clear. For example, I had issues getting my costume. While the shift was at Magic Kingdom, the required costume was available only from the costuming buildings at Epcot and Hollywood Studios. Bobby was with me that day and we tried to go to Hollywood Studios first, but they were so busy that when they saw the blue cast member ID in my hand, they refused to let me park there. We tried to explain to them that I wasn't coming to work, I just needed to get the costume, and we also had dining reservations for lunch. The parking lot staff wouldn't listen and made us go to Epcot's parking lot and then take a bus to Hollywood Studios.

So Bobby and I went to Epcot and decided to go *their* costuming instead of taking a bus to Studios, only to have to come back later to get my car after lunch. We walked from the back of the parking lot to the front gate, assuming there was a backstage entrance to costuming. On the way we passed a giant turtle, which Bobby named and wrote an entire backstory for. When we got to the gate, a confused security guard tried to give us directions to costuming, but essentially we had to walk back to my car and drive to a different location, from which we were finally able to walk to Epcot costuming.

The woman at the front entrance of the building who scanned our IDs told us that we had 15 minutes to get in and out, and if we were any later or tried to sneak into the park, we would be in "serious trouble". This stressed me out, and stressed out Bobby even more, so we rushed to get the costume and then ran out. With that job finally done, we drove back to Hollywood Studios, hiding the blue IDs and posing as guests, and met up with Jessica and Mikey for lunch at the Sci-Fi Dine-in Theater.

It was Hollywood Studios' 25th anniversary. Jessica and her friends had already stocked up on their merchandise and were determined to stay for the special fireworks that night. Bobby and I were content with our silver buttons that we received at the front gate, and as soon as lunch was over we drove to Magic Kingdom. I was running so late that I was trying to change clothes in my car, only to realize at the last minute that I had actually grabbed shorts and not pants. I was worried that they were going to send me home and not let me work the shift—and to make things worse, the shorts didn't fit right, and I had long socks and a long-sleeve shirt. I looked like a total dork and I was furious about it. Luckily, the coordinators didn't care, noting that people everywhere were having costuming issues.

The special events team blocked off an area of Fantasyland in front of the Tea Cups, Winnie the Pooh, Storybook Treats, and a section around the entrance of Mine Train. They filled the area with tables and a full buffet for the guests who were invited to the event. Most of the guests were radio station hosts, blog writers, and other people who would promote the ride for us after the event. There were a few special appearances, as well. Every time we heard whistling the Seven Dwarfs themselves would walk in, along with Snow White. There were some atmosphere actors covered in diamonds who mingled with guests. I thought that I recognized a younger boy who had a guest relations guide walk in with him. I tried not to stare, but I just knew that I had seen him somewhere. I asked another guest relations guide if we had any celebrities in the event, but he just shrugged his shoulders and said he didn't know. It was driving me crazy. I just knew I had seen him somewhere. Suddenly, this little girl with blonde hair ran up to me in a craze. "WHERE IS HE!?"

"Where is who?"

"Bradley Steven Perry!" she screamed.

"I'm sorry, who is that?"

"He's from *Good Luck Charlie*."

"*That's* who that kid was!" I yelled back, matching her energy

"Exactly! Now tell me where he is!"

"I don't know, kiddo, he's in here somewhere. But let me know when you find him."

"Oh, I will," she said very confidently. "Hi, I'm Emaline."

"Hi, Emaline, I'm Cami."

Just then her dad interrupted and told her to "leave the poor girl alone".

"Bye, Cami!"

She danced away, but then came back not 10 minutes later wanting to know why she couldn't get in yet.

"I don't know. The doors were supposed to open at 7."

"It's 7:05," she informed me.

"Just give it a few more minutes," I started to tell her, but then her dad came around the corner to let her know that they were letting them in.

Emaline got her food and then came and sat on a rock next to me and talked to me for a while. She told me that her parents owned a radio station, and that she was a child actress in the making. She had done two movies and a couple of commercials so far. She gave me her autograph so that when she becomes famous I could say "I knew her when". She also promised to take me to Disneyland Paris when she's rich and famous. I still have her autograph.

Toward the end of the evening, Emaline and her parents walked over to me, and they were ecstatic about having met Grumpy Cat during the event. Her dad said, "I've met plenty of celebrities before, but I think I was more excited about meeting that cat than I have anyone else." Emaline's parents gave me their business card and told me that if I ever needed anything to let me know. Then Emaline hugged me goodbye. She was such an inspiring kid. I'll never forget her!

Chapter Ten

On June 14, I celebrated my 20th birthday. It was the first birthday that I had ever spent in a Disney park and I was determined to make the absolute most out of it. I wore a sparkly dress with gold, glittery shoes to match and invited everyone out to Magic Kingdom, encouraging them to dress up as well. Chao Chen, the ICP from China, made me a birthday button on which he wrote my name in Chinese. Andrew and Alex started the day with me; since they lived right next door in Patterson, we drove to the park together and more of my friends joined us as the day wore on. We went to Be Our Guest for lunch, where Belle and the Beast signed me a birthday card. On Main Street, one of my favorite Streetmosphere performers told me I was beautiful and demanded that Andrew and Alex love me. Andrew bought me a princess crown, which Tiana taught me how to wear. Mickey Mouse sang me happy birthday, and the cast member working at the Lunching Pad gave me a free Mickey Pretzel.

In the evening it ended up being just me and Rachel, and then Jamie joined us. Jamie was an ICP from England who I taught how to play Sorcerers of the Magic Kingdom. I saw him every time he came to get his spell cards, and after a few weeks we traded phone numbers. That night we talked on the phone until 5 in the morning and I was definitely developing a little school girl crush on him. When he came out to celebrate my birthday, it was the first time we had hung out in person. I realized very quickly that he actually played for the other team. My bad. Regardless, he was one of the funniest and nicest people that I had ever met. He kept Rachel and me laughing so hard that our sides hurt, at one point dancing around the Confectionery shouting, "It's the queen's birthday!" We all rode Splash Mountain together in our formal wear, and for our picture pose, Jamie and I were taking a selfie. He came back home with us and we watched YouTube videos until finally falling asleep together on the couch. It was the start of a beautiful friendship.

Jamie often came over and watched YouTube videos with me, and he would always come into Magic Kingdom after getting off of work to find me. I'll never forget when he came into the theater telling me that he wanted to self-term because he hated working in the UK Pavilion at Epcot. I didn't hear from him for weeks after that. I was sure he had self-termed until he walked into the theater one night during my shift. I tackled him with tears in my eyes, so thankful that he hadn't left yet. Jamie was one of the most beautiful people that I had ever met, and we always had so much fun together doing things like trying to teach each other how to talk in each other's accents and him teaching me British terms like "posh". He was there during my rough times, and I was there for his. He rooted for me when I was praying to extend my program, and I was always just praying that he would make it through his without self-terming.

Trying to extend my program was one of the most stressful periods of my time here. I wasn't ready to leave yet. Every time I thought about leaving, I thought about Bobby and the castle and Jamie and Mickey Mouse and how I couldn't handle living without them. I was always the outsider in my hometown, but here I felt like I belonged, like I was doing something that mattered. I was genuinely happy for the first time in a very long time. I was worried about my extension because of the reprimand that I had on my record card for attendance.

I tried to talk to Bobby about it, but he was a little more tough on me than I wanted. For good reason, i guess, since Bobby wasn't able to stay after his College Program ended, so he moved back home to New Jersey and then tried to come back. He knew I could do the same, but it wasn't the answer I wanted.

One guest, Kevin, was a regular. He lived in California, but he had an annual pass for Disney World and came here every month. He was an avid Sorcerers of the Magic Kingdom player, and when he came in he looked for me. We developed a friendship over the few months that I was here, and I asked him to pray for my extension. He gave me a hug before he returned home and told me that he knew he would see me again. He said that I was one of the best cast members that he had ever met, and that Disney would be crazy not to not keep me. I was honored by the compliment, but I was still worried.

The Silly Hat Sunday girls wished me luck, too. Kaitlyn and Skylar are twins with annual passers who come to Disney often with their mom and dad. They're an amazingly sweet family, the four of them. The first time I met them was on a Sunday when they were waiting in line for Tiana and I asked about their hats. They told me that every Sunday they wear a silly hat, and never once have they worn the same hat twice. I loved talking to them and hearing their stories; they always knew so much about what was going on in the parks. One night a bunch of us were in Town Square after the parade interacting with guests when the girls showed us the Hidden Mickey on the train station. We were so excited that we stopped almost every guest that walked out to come see this latest discovery.

Despite everyone's encouragement, I was still a nervous, emotional wreck, but I tried to push through the fear and kept thinking about my future with Disney. I noticed that when it came to the leaders on Main Street, almost none of them came to the theater unless it was for an official task like handing out a reprimand. Occasionally we saw them during our closing procedures or for a 4 Keys basics walk, but we didn't have a relationship with them. But I *wanted* a relationship with my leaders; I needed them to know who I was and I needed them to provide a recommendation for me. So I asked to be trained on Parade Audience Control (PAC).

I had picked up untrained PAC shifts before, even though they were anxiety-inducing. There was always so much going on and the PAC cast members never wanted to teach me what to do. There was one time in particular when a PAC cast member told me to have a woman in a wheelchair move out of the way so she could set up the audience control rope. I asked her which way to have the woman move, because I didn't know where the rope went. She instantly became frustrated and told me to just hold the rope so she could move the poor woman, and then later she went around telling other PAC cast members that I was too busy dancing along with the castle show to pay attention and that I had ruined her set up. I was so angry when word got back to me. But that's how it was, every time. I never knew what I was doing and no one wanted to help. As if that weren't enough, I had heard horror stories about PAC cast members being punched in the face by frazzled, violent guests. I was also alarmed by the famous Main Street saying, "Once you go PAC, you never go back", which meant that if I were trained for PAC, I'd probably never be able to work at the theater again (why waste all that PAC training on a temp?). Despite these reservations, I decided to go for it—strictly for networking purposes.

For PAC, I had a brand-new trainer who almost always worked trains. A lot of people felt that her PAC knowledge was outdated, but I chose to trust her and her position as a trainer. I had a small leg up because of the shifts that I had already taken, and as it turned out, I knew a lot more than I thought I did. Once I had the formal training, I was more than confident about everything. (Turns out there are maps that show where the ropes go.) Sure enough, however, once I was in, I was in. I worked a theater shift maybe once every three weeks. It was all PAC, all the time.

And *still* I didn't know about my extension. My roommates and I had talked at the beginning of the program about how we were all going to extend and live together, but now I found myself the only one who wanted to extend. Veronica decided to go back home to Miami; Legs was staying, but moving out with a group of girls she worked with (not that we saw much of her anyway); and Jessica had figured out months ago how to stay with Adam in Chatham and not get caught, so we never saw he, but we knew that she and Adam were going to move back home anyway. The twins were returning to New York and going back to school.

So I was on my own, and I had no idea who I'd be rooming with if I *did* get my extension; and if I didn't get it, what would I do back in Colorado?

The day that extension notices came out me I decided not to think about it and instead took a day off to head for the beach with some girls from work. Aroha, Meg, and Ashley piled into my car and we drove down to the beach at New Smyrna. We spent the day swimming in the ocean and lying on the sand. Finally, I couldn't take it anymore and decided to check my email. There it was, "Congratulations! We look forward to seeing you continue your career with the Walt Disney Company." I collapsed on the beach in relief that I wouldn't have to leave my new home just yet. The girls were thrilled for me, and when we left the beach we walked around the little town and got ice cream. We even stopped at a cute mom-and-pop restaurant for lunch, sitting next to a couple celebrating their 75th wedding anniversary. How amazing is that? I didn't even know people could stay together that long.

When we left the beach we had a 2 ½ hour drive ahead of us to get back home, during one of the worst storms I had ever seen. We ended up in some backwoods town with streets that were completely flooded with things washing away. I had to drive off of the road and over a curb to avoid getting stuck in what seemed like a small lake in the middle of an intersection. It took us forever to find a main road, and every town that we passed on the way to it seemed to have lost power. We eventually got back to the highway, but the rain was so thick that I couldn't see, despite my best efforts, and to make matters worse my gas light had turned on. We pulled over on what we hoped was the side of the road and prayed that the storm would calm down enough for us to be able to move. The lighting and thunder were so loud that the girls in the back seat were screaming. We were scared. Finally, I moved forward enough to get us away from the brunt of the storm and we were able to get gas. I was shaking and scared to drive, and I knew that the girls were equally scared. I put in a CD I have from the Desperation Band, a church band from back home, and let the music soothe us. It was one of the worst drives of my life.

Chapter Eleven

So I was extending. I was relieved, but my mom was disappointed because she hoped that I would come home. For me, it meant six more months save money, find an apartment of my own, and get a real job with Disney. It was more time to get done what I needed to get done, and while I was doing that, I'd also be able to see the Magic Kingdom for Halloween and Christmas. I had put in a housing request for Vista Way because it was the cheapest Disney apartment complex and the people who lived there seemed more social. Plus, Vista was the only complex not to be refurbed with bunk beds. There was just one thing that I didn't consider about extending: I was staying, but none of my friends were. I had to say some goodbyes, a lot of goodbyes, actually. I've never done well with goodbyes. The twins were leaving, Greg was leaving, and most of my friends in the theater and at PAC had chosen to go home as well. The only person that I had left was Bobby, and even that was questionable on a day-to day basis.

Just my luck, though, I made a very poorly timed hello. I met Alyx working in the theater one night, about two weeks or so before the current College program ended. She almost always worked PAC, which is why I had never met her there before. I had seen her around, but we had never really worked together. We hit it off right away in the theater rotunda, and on her break she went down Main Street and bought me treats from Starbucks. We traded numbers, followed each other on every social media platform we had, and walked out at the end of the night together. I had fallen for her pretty much instantly. I guess she had fallen for me, too, because she would come over to my apartment at night and we would sit on the porch and talk. Sometimes we would sit in the theater pit together and clean the FLIK cards (the red cards we use to keep track of wait times) and listen to her music. We had to keep things quiet, just because we worked together, but it made things so much more difficult. She would walk by me and whisper things like "you're beautiful" in my ear, or briefly grab my hand as she passed me. It was so hard to breathe in that theater with her there, though not as hard as it was to breathe when she finally kissed me.

I remember getting so upset that week because I knew she was leaving in a matter of days. We were sitting on the half wall behind the theater when she kissed me mid-sentence. My heart stopped. She was beautiful and I had fallen, hard. I didn't want her to leave. One day I got a Grape Soda pin from the movie *UP* and while she was working Tinker Bell merge, I pulled her into the shrinking hallway and pinned it on the collar of her navy blue vest—but backwards so that she couldn't see what it was yet. "I just wanted you to have something to remember me with when you leave here." I told her not to look at it until I was gone, but just as I reached the door I heard her yell, "Camille!" (I hated that name, but something about the way she said it made me hate it less.) I turned and saw her holding the pin in her hand, smiling at me and mouthing the word "cheeseball". I grinned and slipped out the back of the theater, wishing I could spend every day with her. But then a few days later, she was gone.

Next it was time to say goodbye to Greg. We threw a going-away party for him at Beaches & Cream, with Bobby and Rachel getting the Kitchen Sink, a humongous pile of ice cream scoops and toppings. It was the first time I had seen Bobby in a month after a big fight we had had—over what I don't remember—so it was a little rough at first. But our friendship is one that will always bounce back, no matter what. We lost the battle of the Kitchen Sink and returned to Bobby's apartment sick from ice cream. We all hung out and talked about our favorite Disney moments together, Greg and Rachel curled up on the couch and Bobby and I stood in the kitchen trying to remember why we had that big fight, and whether it meant anything at all. We cried and held each other and apologized, and fell asleep holding hands.

The next morning we got ready to take Greg to the airport. We skipped breakfast, planning on stopping at IHOP on the way to the airport, but when I went to get my car to bring it around, it was gone. I was standing in the parking lot of Bobby's apartment complex exactly where I had parked my car the night before, pressing my panic button frantically, but it was no use—the car wasn't there. I called Bobby with tears in my eyes. "Bobby, my car is gone. I think your complex towed my car." Bobby laughed half-heartedly and told Greg, who started to come up with a plan. So I ran into the front office of the complex and asked where my car went. "Uh, yeah, normally they email us and tell us when they tow a car, but I don't have anything, so it's possible that someone stole your car, but here's the number of the towing business we use if you want to call them, just in case."

I felt a lump in my stomach at the news. When I called Constellation Towing, I was connected to one of the rudest people I had ever talked to in my life, but they had my car. I had to be there at 9:30am with $150 cash. We piled into Bobby's car and drove to Constellation, which was located in a seedy, scary neighborhood. There were signs posted in every yard about how the homeowner was armed, and the signs had pictures of guns on them to prove it. Greg and Rachel held each other in the back seat, terrified. Rachel even began texting people to tell them our location so that someone would know to look for us if she didn't answer her phone. We got to Constellation at around 9, but the gates were all locked and we didn't see any way in or any office outside the gates. So I called the number again and the man yelled at me because he told me to be there at 9:30, not 9, and nobody was going to come help me get the car until 9:30. So we waited, and 9:30 came and still nobody was there, Finally, 10 o'clock came with no response from anybody, and the story was the same at 10:30. Nothing. No response. Now hungry, tired, and out of time, we had to leave to get Greg to the airport.

At the airport, Greg and Rachel walked together holding hands as Bobby and I followed about 15 feet behind. Bobby was more upset than I had ever seen him, continuously crying and talking about how much he would miss Greg. Then we noticed something strange. As Greg and Rachel walked by, people would stop and stare at them. Some even applauded. Nobody could explain it; they're just the perfect couple. The sight made Bobby even more upset; I suspect he wished that he had what Greg and Rachel had. Getting to the gate we joked that this moment felt like the season finale of a bad sitcom, and in a way it did. Greg held and kissed Rachel goodbye, Bobby sobbed and they held each other. I had sworn for weeks that I wouldn't cry when I said goodbye to Greg, but I did. Rachel and Greg were going to see each other again in just a few weeks, but Bobby and I didn't know when we'd see him again, or if we ever would.

We went back to the tow yard where they made us wait another two hours to get my car. At this point, it was 5:00pm and I started my shift at 6:15. There was no way I was going to make it into work on time, not being stuck all the way out here and still having to take Rachel back home and get my costume. Still, I was going to try. When I had stopped just outside the tow gate to plug my phone into the car charger, I got a knock on my window. I looked up to find Bobby, with an apologetic look on his face, telling me that his car was dead.

"That's it. I'm calling in," I said, giving up on the day. I called Disney and told them I wasn't going to make it into work. I pulled my car around to Bobby's car and dug out the jumper cables. We started to google the instructions for jump-starting a car when the tow yard worker came out and offered to help, clearly laughing at our cluelessness. He got the car jumped for us, and we finally made it home safely.

A week later I got my housing assignment to move apartments for my extension. I had been assigned a three-bedroom apartment at Vista Way. I packed my car on August 2 and made the short trip to my new, dingy apartment, not knowing any of the girls that I would be living with. I found my new room with its tiny closet and overhead light that barely worked. We had two refrigerators, hardwood floors, only two bathrooms, and a musty smell coming from the vents. What a downgrade from Patterson. I tried to make the most of it. My roommates seemed like very relaxed girls, a little more promiscuous and open than what I was used to, but at least they were nice. Only five of us moved in that first day, and we were all CPs who had extended.

The next day while I was sleeping a girl with a suitcase poked her head into my room: "Um, hi. I'm Jacqueline. I think I'm supposed to stay here?"

I pointed to the empty bed on the other side of the room and said "that's yours", and then rolled over and fell back asleep. I officially met her later in the day and found out that she was just like my friends from back home, had a serious boyfriend that she couldn't wait to see again, and had brought barely anything with her. Rachel and Liz were moving out that same day and offered to give me a lot of their stuff that they had planned on throwing out, so I took Jacqueline with me and we got full bed sets, lamps, mattress pads, probably 20 pillows, dishes, and food. It made Jacqueline feel better, seeing as she had brought so little.

A few days later I was working the Electrical Parade in front of the firehouse, and near the end of the parade I turned around and found Rachel and Liz in my section. After the parade ended they told me that they were leaving that second, and this was goodbye. We all cried, holding each other on the corner of Main Street, knowing we would see each other again, but not sure when. I knew I was saying goodbye to two of the best friends that I had down here. Then they were gone, and I felt lost, not sure how to make new friends after all of these people that I loved so much had left.

About two weeks later, I woke up early one morning to take Bobby to the airport. Being lazy with my hair, I threw it all into a beanie and snuck quietly out of my apartment. In front of my porch were two boys cuddling on top of a car. I smiled, thinking they were cute, until I realized who it was.

"Jamie! You foxy little Brit! What are you doing out here this early in the morning?" I joked, sneaking up behind him.

"Cami!" He came down from the car and tackled me in a large hug. Excited, not knowing that this was the building where I now lived, he was thrilled to learn that we were neighbors. He introduced me to the boy he was with as Landon, who lived in the apartment next to mine. Landon was a character performer and often appeared in the Electrical Parade, holding the canopy. We said that we would have to look for each other at the next parade. I hugged them both and left to get Bobby.

On my next parade shift I didn't spot Landon, but I did see him on the Westclock shuttle bus that night leaving work. He told me about a really good tea that he likes to make, and said that he would make it for me sometime soon. The next week, I saw him in both parades that ran that night and he waved to me each time. After work I went out to Steak 'n Shake with some people from work, and when I returned home in the middle of the night I was greeted to a cup of tea sitting on my kitchen table, along with a drawing of Rapunzel. On the back of the drawing was a note from Landon, telling me that he was happy to see me in both parades and that he hoped I enjoyed the tea, assuring me that he would see me again soon. I was thrilled. I thought it was such a sweet little act of kindness. The next morning I went and knocked on his door to thank him, and we spent some time together watching television.

After that, it was permanent. Landon and I were attached at the hip. We were always together before and after work, sometimes even driving to work in the same car. Often I got him dinner and would meet him at his house, spending the night sitting on his bed watching *Girls*. He came over one day and met my roommates, Tori and Amanda, and hit it off with them right away. We all just clicked and spent a lot of time together. The three of us began to notice that we had a connection with the novel *The Perks of Being a Wallflower*. Jamie referred to us as his "Perks Friends" and I felt like I was a part of something special.

One night I went with Jamie, Landon, and Tori to Waffle House after work, where we met one of the employees, Kristoff. We spent the entire night there joking around with Kristoff, and before we left I traded phone numbers with him. He had taken quite the crush on Jamie, but Jamie wasn't interested. We went home and Tori and I lay in my bed, Jamie and Landon in Amanda's bed, and we talked and joked until the sun came up, and the next thing we knew it was six in the morning, which only meant one thing—Starbucks was open. So we went to Starbucks in our pajamas, except for Landon, who was wearing a makeshift Snuggie and Mickey Mouse slippers. Slap happy and tired at Starbucks, we stormed in making too much noise, but the employees loved Landon and Jamie, thinking them hilarious and adorable, which they were. The two of them fed off each other's energy and continued to energize each other as the morning wore on.

After we left Starbucks, we were in my car stopped at a red light, and I honestly cannot tell you what happened next, or why I had an empty container of laundry detergent in the back seat of my car. All I know is that I heard Jamie screech out of terror as the laundry detergent launched from the back of the car, hit the front window, bounced off of the dashboard a few times before turning on the windshield wipers, and then fell into Tori's lap. It was slightly terrifying, but it caused everyone to laugh so hard that we couldn't breathe. It was one of my favorite moments that the four of us shared, and it's one that was talked about for months.

But then things started to change. I was seeing more and more of Landon and less and less of Jamie. And Jamie and Landon started to fight, and they fought, and fought, and then fought some more. I found myself caught in the middle and didn't know how to get out. Jamie started to get it in his head that Landon and I were getting together and saying bad things about him all the time, and I couldn't convince him otherwise. Eventually, Landon told Jamie that he didn't want him in his life anymore, because he brought too much drama.

That's when Jamie exploded, and I got the brunt of it. I received the most hurtful message that I have ever received from a friend. Jamie told me that I was a terrible person who ruined friendships, and that he didn't believe I was even humane. Landon and I both tried to tell Jamie that I didn't have anything to do with Landon's decision, but he wouldn't hear it. He wanted nothing more to do with me. I stayed the night at Landon's, lying in his bed crying because I had lost Jamie. I tried so hard to get Jamie to forgive me, but he wouldn't, and every time he walked past me and Landon on the porch, he kept a straight face and stormed past us, unphased, never answering as I called his name. Eventually, I stopped trying. I just let him walk by as I kept my head down.

Chapter Twelve

Before I knew it, my entire life was work, Landon, and my roommates. I was sleeping in Landon's bed every night. We moved my mattress pad into his room, and I kept clothes at his house. We went grocery shopping together and kept all the food in his fridge. I was working more than ever and picking up as many shifts as I could. I was working as much as 60–70 hours a week, and it was starting to wear down my health.

I was thankful, though, because I was finally making friends at work. Most of the time I was with Josh and Spencer, two guys who cared a lot about me and were always there to make me laugh. No matter where their positions were, they always came to find me for a hug before the parade started.

Then there were support shifts. Support is operating the FastPass+ viewing areas for the parades and fireworks, and it generally means standing around all day and taking as long as 4-hour breaks, depending on who was coordinating. The main joy of working support shifts? Getting to watch Dream Along with Mickey three times in the same day. My friend Tobias and I would always dance and sing along like it was us on the stage. Our favorite part was the princess scene, in which Tobias would waltz me around the FastPass area as we sang along. Guests would often film and take pictures of us, or come tell us later that we were "the real stars of Disney".

In particular, I loved support shifts because they were always good for getting to know other cast members. For instance, Tran. Tran was one of our coordinators who worked support more often than the others. During these support shifts, Tran and I would talk. He told me stories about his time in the service and his family and how after all he'd been through this was his "fun job". At the end of the day, nothing made Tran happier than his family. It didn't take long until I was looking at Tran as a serious role model, and after some time I started referring to him as "Uncle Tran". He was always there to give me a hug when I needed one, or to get me a rain poncho on the days I had forgotten mine and Florida had turned against me. Our friendship developed over the months that I was there, and he told me that he was able to tell me things that he hadn't told anyone in over a decade, and I was honored. Even on the bad days, I knew that I could always go to Tran.

The bad days do happen on this program, as much as we want to believe that everything here is made out of pixie dust and has the power of dreams, and although it feels like we're trapped in the safe "Disney Bubble", somewhere out there is the real world, and it finds its way in.

One day between parades I was down in the break room with my friends when I got a text from my friend back home, Jenny, asking if I was still friends with a boy named Brennan on Facebook. Brennan was my first boyfriend, in middle school, and he had recently joined the Marines. I told her I was, although when I asked why, she just instructed me to go look at his Facebook page. I thought maybe he had posted some dorky picture of him and my seventh grade self. But what I found was much worse. Brennan had been killed in a car accident on the way home to his family. I dropped my phone and ran out of the break room and down the Utilidors until I didn't want to run anymore and I collapsed between some boxes against the wall and cried.

A manager found me a few minutes later and asked if I was okay, I told her what happened and that I was fine, I just needed to be away from the break room. After a few minutes I went back and my friends looked at me like they were scared and I told them that I had lost a friend, and it just surprised me. I apologized for worrying them and left to go to the PAC room to wait for the meeting. The manager who had found me crying in the Utilidors and had told my coordinators, who asked if I wanted to go home. While I appreciated the concern, I didn't want the attention. I wanted to stay here, on Main Street, U.S.A., surrounded by people, not sitting alone in my dingy Vista Way apartment.

I made the right decision, because that night I met the guests that I will never forget.

Whenever people ask me what it's like to work at Disney, or what my favorite memory is, this is what I tell them. I was working in Town Square when an older woman in an ECV (one of those motorized wheelchairs) flags me down. She was behind about three rows of people who were all sitting on the ground. She asked me if they would stand when the parade started. I told her that they might or they might not; they have no reason to stand, since they have front-row views, but there's no way to tell what guests will do during a parade. I noticed her demeanor change and she became slightly frantic. She told me that she was here ten years ago, still in an ECV, and had tried to watch the parade in front of the castle. That area is always packed for the Electrical Parade. She said that she couldn't see the parade well and when it was halfway through, she had a medical need to get to the bathroom ASAP, but nobody would move for her. She was bumping guests with her ECV and screaming for them to move, but no one would. I believed every word of it. I knew how these crowds get. Then she started to cry. She told me that since then, she had promised her granddaughter, Chloe, that she would bring her here to see the Electrical Parade. Today was Chloe's 11th birthday. I learned that the lady in the ECV had just been diagnosed with cancer, and that tonight would likely be her last opportunity to see the parade.

My heart broke all over again. I felt it drop to the bottom of my stomach as she sat in her ECV and wept. I ran to a manager and begged him to let me move Chloe and her grandmother to VIP viewing. He seemed annoyed, as the parade would start in just four minutes, and he told me to hurry. I went back for the grandmother and started screaming for people to move out of the way. I got her to the area right in front of the Emporium and asked where Chloe was. "In the Confectionery buying herself candy. She's wearing a Happy Birthday Chloe button." I raced over to the Confectionery and ran around the store yelling for Chloe, asking cast members if they had seen her, but nobody had. I ran back to where I had originally met her grandmother and asked the people sitting there if anyone had seen her, but nobody knew what I was talking about. I heard the parade music start and my stomach dropped again. Then I turned around just in time to see Chloe standing on the sidewalk outside the confectionery.

"Chloe! Chloe, sweetheart, I moved your grandmother to a different area. Can you come with me?"

She followed me over to where her grandmother now was, and I got her there the second the gates opened, with Tinker Bell there to greet them.

"We get to watch the parade from here?" Chloe asked me

"Yes, ma'am! Just for you!"

"Yay! Thank you so much!" she turned around and waved to Tinker Bell, immediately entranced with all the lights.

Her grandmother grabbed me by the arm and pulled me down to her ECV, kissing my cheeks, crying, saying over and over again, "Bless you. Bless you. This was my final wish. Thank you so much. Bless you. Thank you."

I told her that I was so happy to help, and to enjoy the parade, and that it was an honor to meet her.

I finished that night with a broken heart, ready to go home, but I knew I made a difference for Chloe and her grandmother, and that was all that mattered. However, as the next few days went on, that family was all that I could think about. I felt guilty for getting to watch this parade every night. But, by seeing the parade so often, I had come to almost hate it. I was tired of it. And I was tired that the worst guests were the ones who seemed to come to this parade, and they always caused problems and never seemed to be happy. Yet here was this woman, who loved the parade so much that she had promised her granddaughter for 10 years that she would bring her to it, and that's how she chose to celebrate the end of her life. The feeling weighed on me for days and every night that I heard the music and saw Tinker Bell I thought about Chloe and I felt even worse.

I talked to several cast members about it, and many of them consoled me and told me that the first time they met a family like that it had an effect on them, too. During Traditions, the formal course all cast members must take before they can work for Disney, the instructor told us that people come here to celebrate the end of their lives, and I remembered from my time in Housekeeping that some people come here to die, but you never understand it until you meet those families. What bothered me the most was that many of the cast members in whom I confided rolled their eyes and said, "She was probably just faking it to get a better parade seat. People make things up all the time." It was astonishing to me how many cast members, especially in PAC, had turned bitter. I understood why, because PAC involved fighting with guests night after night, but this is Walt Disney World. Aren't we supposed to be happy and magical here? Why are so many people that work here being taught to despise and distrust people? I didn't want to be that way. So I turned my mind around, and I smiled every time that I heard the Electrical Parade music and I waved to Tinker Bell each night as she passed.

One night I was talking to one of the Peter Pan character performers, discussing how the rain that day had caused every other parade to be cancelled. When this happens, entertainment fights to put on the Electrical Parade as much as they can. They just want to give the guests *something*. He scoffed and said, "I'm sorry, but this parade is not going to cheer anyone up."

"You'd be surprised, actually."

"What do you mean?"

"Believe it or not, some people really love this parade."

"Nobody loves this parade," he laughed. "It's so old!"

I told him the story about Chloe and her grandmother and added that the Electrical Parade is my mom's absolute favorite thing in all of Walt Disney World. He thought for a moment and told me that I had really helped his attitude. He gave me a hug and walked out, and later that night gave me a friendly wave from the pirate ship.

Chapter Thirteen

Halloween Season was perhaps my favorite part of the program. I've never had so much fun as I did working the Mickey's Not-So-Scary Halloween Parties, which started on September 1. There were fifty of us crammed in the girls' bathroom changing into our very festive costumes which consisted of purple skirts, green-and-yellow-striped shirts, and candy corn aprons, with a purple bat headband. The other girls all named their bats, determined to keep theirs for the entire season, but I never jumped into that game. The first party I worked was a support shift. We don't use FastPass for the Halloween parties, but there was a separate ticketed dessert party, the Villains Soiree, which included a sweets meal with the villains in the castle and special seating for the parades and fireworks. We were in charge of the special seating area. It was the easiest shift I had ever worked. We spent hours talking to guests and admiring everyone's costumes, amazed with people's creativity. We also started a game called Count the Elsas, but here's the thing: there are too many to count.

I was so excited to see the Boo To You Parade the first time it rolled down Main Street that I could hardly sit still. Along with three other PAC cast members and our coordinator, Cesar, we sat on the ground next to the entrance of our viewing area and watched in awe as the parade came by. I was overwhelmed with excitement when I saw the Winnie the Pooh characters at the front and fell in love when Eeyore came and kissed me as he danced by wearing his Halloween mask. Aladdin pointed at me and blew me a kiss. The ballroom dancers from the Haunted Mansion gave me goosebumps, and I fell in love with the villains. Except for the hyenas, of course—they scare me.

I was becoming very good friends with a security guard, Ian, who undoubtedly liked me despite how often I tried to defuse it. He happened to be working in the park that night, which wasn't often, and he came to watch the fireworks show, HalloWishes, with me. We normally are not allowed to stop and watch the fireworks. It makes us look lazy when we're supposed to be controlling walkways and directing guests, but that night I couldn't help it. HalloWishes was the most amazing thing that I had ever seen. From the opening song of "When you hear the knell of a requiem bell" to the "Scream-along" at the very end, HalloWishes took no time at all in stealing a big part of my heart.

The more I worked the Halloween parties, the more I wished that every night was a Halloween night. While I was getting over wearing the costume, I was never over the fun.

One night at Landon's apartment I was introduced to Jared, a boy with the most beautiful eyes that I had ever seen, who was an Aladdin character performer. Every night that there was a Halloween party I was always guaranteed three things. First, Aladdin would find me and either give me a hug or a kiss on the hand. Second, Eeyore would pick on me. I never knew who was Eeyore on those nights, but during every parade he would come by, point at me as if to say "I found you!", and then come running up with hugs and kisses. One night during a parade I was kneeling on the ground so the guests behind me could see. Aladdin came over to kiss my hand and the next thing I knew I was face-first on the ground. Somebody had tackled me. I rolled over, confused, and then Eeyore was smothering my face with kisses before running away. I remember lying flat out on Main Street thinking, 'Eeyore just tackled me to the ground. So that's how my day is going.'

The third thing that I was always guaranteed was Phineas and Ferb and the "Creepa Crew". They were one of our pre-parade acts, along with the Headless Horseman. Phineas and Ferb would show up with their hip-hop dance crew and invite kids to come out and dance with them. Cast members could also dance, with one condition: we can't go out alone. I would always get kids who were waiting for the parade to start pumped up by telling them, "You know who's coming out in five minutes, right? Phineas and Ferb! We're going to have a giant dance party and get Halloween candy! You're going to come dance with me, right? Right?" I usually brought out a couple of kids with me, sometimes holding their hands as they danced. Others would forget about me and go straight for Phineas and Ferb. Regardless, each dance party was a blast, and it was my break from a stressful day. Each time they came around I would always give Ferb, one of my favorite characters, a great big hug. It got to the point where Ferb recognized me and would always make sure to find me and come hug me before dancing down the street. Some nights he even smuggled Halloween candy into my apron pocket before disappearing.

I even loved working in the theater during the Halloween parties. We had a special card for the Sorcerers of the Magic Kingdom, and Mickey Mouse dressed up in his Halloween costume told us Halloween jokes. One of my favorite pictures with Mickey is from the night I worked the Halloween party with him.

My friendship with Landon was better than ever, though Jamie still wouldn't talk to us. Landon was spending every day with me and my roommates; some days I would come home to him sleeping on my couch. Frozen Summer Fun at Hollywood Studios had been extended, and Landon was cast to hang out with the Ice Cutters for the parade. One day he offered to take me to work with him, and it was such an incredible experience. We woke up early, stopping at Starbucks on the way, and pulled into the cast parking lot in our sweats like queens. He took me through the entire Entertainment department. I got to see how the dancers' costumes were prepared and taken care of, and what it took for the characters to ready themselves for the parade. Afterward, I sat in the front row of the parade route and got special attention from the Ice Cutter himself. He made me feel like I was the most important girl in the world.

Landon had that effect on people. He could make you feel like you were the only person in the world worth talking to, and he did it so effortlessly. For the boys he dated he drew pictures or did something special or cute to stand out. He often referred to himself as a "people pleaser". I would've done anything for Landon, and I felt like I did a lot. Most days, Landon did not have any money. I was always spotting him money or giving him food, driving him to work. Whatever he needed, I wanted to be there for him. Landon's roommate, Sam, and I were becoming close, too. Sam worked on Soarin' and was hands-down the best flight attendant you could ask for. Sam was always there to cheer me up if I needed him, often holding me and singing "Don't Cry". To this day I don't know where that song came from or what half the words were, but he and Landon would sing it to me and it meant the world to me. Tori and Amanda were in love with him, thinking that he was the most stunning man in Vista Way (which he probably was), but I never had feelings for him. I just thought he was an amazing person who loved Aladdin. A lot.

Then I met Vince. I actually had met Vince back in the spring when he was training in the theater, I told him that he looked like Captain America and then never really saw him again until now. We were working together in the plaza when my roommates Tori and Amanda stopped by to say hello. They saw him and immediately asked if he was single so he could date them. I told them I would find out, and after they left I immediately asked him if he was single, and he said he was. After that we started to talk a little, but not much, since he was kind of quiet. As the weeks went by Vince and I began to talk more and more, and I was developing a bit of a crush since he was, well, flawless. Physically flawless.

One night during a PAC meeting I was sitting next to him, not even pretending to pay attention to anything else. I asked Vince stupid questions like his favorite color (yellow), his favorite music, his favorite movie, his favorite type of pizza—the important questions for getting to know a person. We talked all the time. Finally, I shot him a text: "Hey. I think you're cute and rad and really funny and if you ever wanted to take me on a date I would be okay with it." His response was something nice about how he just wanted to be friends. But that was all it took; it was that easy. Our friendship started there, and it consisted of pizza, Netflix, books, music, and his cat, Tiffany. Eventually, he introduced me to his friend Rey, who sometimes drove up to spend a few days at Disney with us. Rey was pretty great, too. I'm lucky to know the both of them.

In late September I went back home to go visit my family for my little sister's birthday. I couldn't have been more negative about the trip. I was glad to see my family, but I had engraved into my head that I couldn't stand Colorado. It was no place for me; it was too cold, but more importantly it wasn't Disney, so I didn't want to be there. I complained about everything—the cold, the cats, the people, the bike lanes. While I was gone, Landon called me every night to tell me that he missed me. Some nights Tori and Amanda or Sam would be on the phone with him as well, all on speaker telling me they missed me and wanted me to come home. I couldn't wait to get back.

When I did return to Orlando, I couldn't have been any happier to see Vista Way. I knew that this place was my real home and that there was no other place for me. Landon, Sam, and my roommates were my family now, and I didn't want to go anywhere else.

But then things started to change. I knew for a while that Tori and Amanda didn't care for the girl I shared a room with, Jacqueline. I wasn't sure why, except that maybe she was quieter than they were. I don't even think they knew why. They just liked having someone to be mean to. Jacqueline sometimes slept talked in her sleep. It was usually silly things like, "Where are the puppies?" or "The butterflies are really loud tonight." But one night I came home and Jacqueline rolled over and asked, "Cami, do you hate me?"

"What?"

"I know you hate me."

"Jackie, what are you talking about? I don't hate you."

"I can just hear you guys talking about me through the walls sometimes."

"Jackie, go back to sleep."

"Okay." She giggled a little and then rolled back over.

Later in the day when she woke up I was washing dishes and spotted her in the hall.

"Jackie, do we need to talk?"

"About what?"

"Do you remember anything that you said to me last night?"

"No, I don't."

"You do know that I don't hate you, right?"

"Oh. I just. Oh." Jackie sat on her bed with her face in her hands and started to cry. She then started to tell me about how she could hear Tori and Amanda talking about her through the walls at night and how she was always just trying to stay out of their way so that she wouldn't make them upset. She told me that they were the reason she went out all of the time and stayed away from home. She cooked dinner at her friend's house so that she wouldn't upset them. I felt terrible.

That night I asked Amanda and Tori to meet me on the front porch. I told them that they can say whatever they wanted, just not to do it in the house where she could hear them. I told them that I wasn't about making someone feel unwelcome in their own home.

"Yeah, well, I'm not in this program to make friends, so I don't care," was Amanda's response. Tori agreed. Frustrated and disappointed, I went to Landon's to stay the night for the last time, deciding that I should be in my apartment every night from now on so that Jacqueline wouldn't feel like she was completely alone. For the most part I think it helped, though Jacqueline did have friends elsewhere, and she often spent time with them.

I wasn't as fortunate. I was spending all of my time with Landon and my roommates, as my other friendships began to falter. After a while, things started to change in the group, as well. Landon, for instance, was spending more time with Amanda than he was me. He asked me if I was jealous and I told him that I wasn't, which was true. I was glad that they were friends and I was glad that we could all be friends together. I loved having everyone at home to play games and watch horror movies. It was when they started excluding me that I began to get a little upset, but I chose to shake it off as much as I could.

At one point, I asked Bobby if he wanted to go to a Halloween party with me at Magic Kingdom. He didn't, and told me to "take Leonard, or whatever his name is." His comment sparked an argument between us, and with Landon sitting next to me on the couch, he bore witness to the entire thing. Later that night, without my knowledge, Landon found Bobby on my Facebook list and sent him his opinion of the matter. It started the biggest fights I ever had with Bobby. He didn't talk to me for some time, and when next we worked a theater shift together, he wanted nothing to do with me. We stood in the Tinker Bell Shrinking Hall and fought, and then we went to the pit where we first met and fought, we fought in the rotunda, in stroller parking, on the patio, up and down Town Square. We fought and we fought and we fought about any obstacle our friendship had encountered to that point, but came out of it back to normal. I guess that was the comfort of having Bobby's friendship, and why I dealt with all the fighting, because I knew that no matter what, we'd get over it.

I ended up not going to the Halloween party with Landon or with Bobby, but instead with one of my high school friends, Katie, who had flown in from Colorado. It was great to see her again. We spent the morning at Epcot where Katie fell in love with Ellen's Energy Adventure, and then we spent the evening at Magic Kingdom. Katie dressed as Ursula and I as a hipster version of Merida. We danced with Phineas and Ferb, gawked at the parade, and even got a surprise meet and greet with my favorite villain, Dr. Facilier.

Not long after Katie's visit came the end of the Halloween season. On October 31 we all put on our candy corn aprons and wore our bat bows for the last time. I was working the west side of the parade, waiting in our "park clear" positions for the signal that the parade was about to begin, when a little girl ran straight at me pointing at my head and yelling, "What is the name of your bat?!" I froze, realizing that I never named mine, and gave her the first name that came to mind: "Geoffrey!". She covered her mouth with her hands as though I had just told her something appalling and whispered, "That's beautiful." Then she ran off in the opposite direction. I laughed so hard I could barely contain myself.

I was sad to see the Halloween season end. The Headless Horseman rode past us for the last time, followed by the Creepa Crew. At the end of our dance I looked at Ferb and we both dropped our arms in realization. "Ferb...," I said, in a sad tone. He ran to me and we both held each other for a long time, Ferb blowing kisses in my ear and me saying, "Thank you for everything Ferb. I love you." Ferb ran to a dancer, grabbed a handful of candy, and came and shoved it in my apron pocket, then gave me another hug. It may sound childish, but tears started to fill my eyes. "We have to go now, Ferb," a dancer said to him, but he didn't move. "Ferb, are you okay?" she asked him, but Ferb just looked at me, waved, and then put his head down in sadness and walked away. Out of all of the amazing character interactions that I experienced on this program, the one with Ferb is what I will cherish the most after I've left this place.

The last run of the parade was perfect. Aladdin and Eeyore both gave me hugs as usual, the flag pirates made faces at me, and Jack Sparrow gave me his drunken salute. It was no different than what we'd done throughout the season, except this time around I cherished it just a bit more. We broke down the parade as quickly as we could and literally ran backstage. After the parade reached its endpoint in Town Square, all the characters came and hugged those of us in PAC. Everyone was crying and congratulating each other, and thanking each other for all of their hard work. We got surplus amounts of Halloween candy, and we even got to meet the Haunted Mansion dog, Jolene. It was an amazing night and the perfect end to the season. I'll never forget that feeling we all had at the end of the parade that night, or the way I felt after seeing HalloWishes for the last time. Not So Scary will always be my favorite Disney event.

The Halloween parties might not be so scary, but Tigger is. Don't get me wrong, I love Tigger, he's always been one of my favorite characters, and he was one of the most memorable characters from my first day in the Magic Kingdom. But now Tigger is *really* memorable, though the feeling he brings are ones of dread, not love.

One night I was walking through the Utilidors during a theater shift on my way to the Christmas Shoppe. On my way there I have to pass by the Crystal Palace break room, which is no big deal, since I pass by their break room all the time. The Crystal Palace has character dining with Pooh, Piglet, Eeyore, and Tigger. Every now and then I see them sitting in their break room, but they always keep to themselves; character performers are like that. But this night I found Tigger standing in the middle of a Utilidor hallway by himself. Just standing there. I remember thinking to myself, "What is Tigger doing out here? Why isn't he in his break room?" But I chose to ignore it and kept walking in his direction. That was mistake number one. Even when a Pargo came down the hall and I watched Tigger try to climb on it as it was moving, I still chose to still ignore it, thinking, "Tigger is just being a troll today. Okay." That was my second mistake.

The third mistake happened when Tigger saw me. I was hoping he wouldn't, but he did. He saw me and he stared. A cold, hard stare as I continued to walk toward him. When I got about ten feet away from him he put his arms out, as if to invite me in for a hug. My naive, magical self thought, "Oh, how cute! Surprise meet and greet with Tigger! Yay!" So I started toward him asking out loud, "What are you doing down here, Tigger?" Tigger didn't change expression or move at all. Though it was strange, I kept approaching.

When I got about three feet away from Tigger, he began to move his arms up and down slowly. I didn't know what he was trying to get across there, but that's when I made my final mistake. I chose to try to hug him anyway. Saying out loud again, "Are we doing a slow motion hug? What's going on, Tigger?" When I went to put my arms around him, my face immediately in front of his, he let out the most terrifying and horrific growl that I have ever heard. The growl scared me so badly, mostly because I wasn't expecting it, that it caused me to scream and then immediately start crying. Tears poured down my face.

I ran, but Tigger chased. He wasn't running, but had switched into full-on *Walking Dead* mode. He was limping, had his arms in front of him, and was growling like a zombie as he chased me in circles around the hall. About this time, I noticed that the men who were driving the Pargo from earlier stopped to watch the show and were laughing at me, yelling, "How could you be afraid of him? It's just Tigger!" In between sobs I called back, "He's trying to kill me!"

I continued to run and Tigger continued to chase. At one point I was yelling at Tigger "Stop it! You're ruining every childhood memory I have ever had! Stop it right now!" That's when I ran into a wall, which Tigger pinned me to. He had both paws on my head, holding me against the wall, his face inches from mine and growling, just growling. I remember in my head thinking, "This is it. This is how I'm going to die. This cast member has snapped and he's just going to snap my neck and they're going to find me dead down here and nobody will know and there will be no fingerprints either."

I looked out of the corner of my eye. The men in the Pargo had left. It was just me and Tigger. Now, this was not my proudest moment ever, but I accepted my death. I just closed my eyes and waited for him to kill me. Instead of snapping my neck, Tigger instead gave me a giant kiss on the forehead and then ran into his break room and slammed the door.

I wiped the tears from my eyes and began to walk away, still in shock about what had just happened to me. About 30 seconds or so later I heard way-too-loud footsteps behind me. My heart dropped, I turned around to see the orange-and-black giant behind me again. All I could do was yell, "TIGGER! WHY!?" His response was dropping his arms to his sides and running back into his break room. I sprinted to the end of the hall to the staircase before he could come back. I ran into a Merchandise cast member who was about to go down the same way I had just came from. She asked if I was okay, noticing that I was trying to wipe the tears from my eyes. I just told her "Be careful going back there. Tigger has gone mad."

"What? What are you talking about?"

"Tigger. Tigger has gone crazy and he's trying to kill me."

"Uh, okay. I can't tell if you're kidding or...?"

"Not kidding," I told her, still wiping my eyes. "Just be careful going down there."

I can only imagine what was going on in her head. I wonder if she met the zombie version of Tigger or if I was the only one to be so blessed. Either way, it's almost a year later and I still can't look at Tigger the same way.

Chapter Fourteen

With the end of the season of scary and not-so-scary things, came the Christmas season. Now *that* was a trip. While there was no Horseman or Creepa Crew to worry about, we were blessed with the castle lighting. In the past, Cinderella and the Fairy Godmother would attend the castle lighting ceremony once each night, and the Fairy Godmother would use her magic to light the Christmas lights on the castle. This year, however, there was a change. Anna and Elsa were to light the castle, along with their friends Kristoff and Olaf. Amazing, right? And not just once, but *twice* each night.

It was a nightmare.

I hated the castle lighting, for several reasons, but mostly because it was poorly timed. On nights that we had a Christmas party, the first lighting would happen about 15 minutes before we closed the park to day guests. So then we would have thousands of people clustered in front of the castle, being told they needed to leave, but not wanting to leave because they thought they had claimed a stellar seat for the fireworks. By the time we got the park cleared of anyone who didn't have a Christmas party ticket, the parade route was over-filled, just in time for the second castle lighting, which happened 15 minutes before the parade stepped off. So again, we had thousands of people camped out in front of the castle who want to watch the parade and "don't want to wait for the second parade because we have kids who can't stay awake that late", and I had nowhere to send them, nowhere to suggest watching the parade other than staying for the second showing. I had never gotten yelled at more by guests or gotten into more fights with guests than I did on Christmas party nights. Naturally, most nights they had me in the Plaza. It was miserable. Every night was four hours straight of screaming and fighting. I was so busy arguing that I never once was able to enjoy the parade or the fireworks myself.

Christmas was turning me into a bitter person. I was starting to resent going to work, and I was starting to hate people in general. No matter what day it was, I didn't want to be there, I didn't even want to think about the plaza, and I swore that if I heard Anna say "Elsa! Why don't you use your Frozen Fractal powers to cover the castle in ice and snow?" one more time, I was going to hit something.

The only good thing that came out of the Christmas season was getting to watch them film for the Christmas Day Parade. Imagine my surprise when I found that it did not actually take place on Christmas day...magic ruined! Becky and I went to the filming along with another Becki, who worked with us in the theater, and her kids. We arrived early in the morning and landed a front- row view near Casey's Corner. Watching them film stressed me out, because PAC wasn't allowed to be in the streets. I was just *waiting* for someone to run across the street or for a kid to run up to a character, but amazingly it never happened. We were there during the third day of filming, and saw the *Frozen*, *Big Hero 6*, and Phineas and Ferb segments, as well as some other floats that seemed to be thrown in here and there. Robin Roberts and Tim Tebow were the hosts. Roberts was adorable; I remember her walking down the street wearing her professional clothes and Mickey slippers and saying "Oh, hey!"

Ariana Grande was one of the performers at the filming we attended. Her trailer was parked in our backstage PAC area, and they had it surrounded with walls so we couldn't see her. We all laughed when we saw it. I'm not the biggest fan of Ariana Grande in the first place, and besides that, celebrities come through the Magic Kingdom all the time. When they filmed an episode of *The Middle* here, the cast had all their trailers parked in the back, and it didn't phase anyone. One of the actors from that show would sit at the smoking table with cast members and smoke with them on their breaks.

It was raining the day that they were filming Ariana's performance, so Disney asked her to wear flats or sneakers for her safety. She refused to go out until they let her wear her stilettos. Disney had to send out people to towel dry the stage so that she could walk on it in her heels. Ridiculous.

It was around this time that I started being friends with a co-worker, Justin, who had an insane girlfriend. I couldn't spend 5 minutes with Justin without her calling and screaming at him. She was getting on my last nerve quickly, and I was starting to fight back. One night when Justin and I went to Waffle House after work, I planted a status on my Facebook to see if she was looking at my page, and sure enough, she was. I chose to ignore her after that, I was done walking on eggshells. So after work Justin and I would go to Waffle House and hang out with Kristoff, who often blessed us with free food, and would often stay there until the sun came up. One night Justin and I even left and drove around town for an hour, only to end up back at Waffle House with Kristoff again. Whenever I was having a hard time, I would call Kristoff and ask if he was working; if he was, I would just say, "I'll be there in 5 minutes," and by the time I got there, Kristoff would be waiting for me with a pecan waffle and a vanilla coffee drink. We would sit outside Waffle House and drink coffee, smoke cigarettes, and talk about life. Then we found the song "Coffee and Cigarettes" by Never Shout Never, which has a line about going to Waffle House. Undoubtedly this song was about our lives and sometimes we would sit outside in the parking lot and sing it together. By the end of my program, I knew not only Kristoff but everyone who worked at that Waffle House on a first-name basis. As weird as it sounds, they were like family.

Not long after, Justin broke up with his girlfriend, and was spending more time with me. I never suspected that there was any romantic interest between us until one night after work I got to my car, only to find a heart taped to my window with the words saying, "Come get lost with me. I'll be at Waffle House." It was almost two in the morning. I couldn't believe that this was happening. So I drove straight to Waffle House, still wearing my red, green, and candy cane PAC costume, where I spotted Justin sitting on top of his car waiting for me. We ate at Waffle House and talked to Kristoff until the sun came up, but on the inside I was worried about Justin having feelings for me. After all, he had broken up with his girlfriend only a few days before, and they still lived together.

About a week later, Justin told me that he wanted to spend a day hanging out together, and that he wanted to "make it special". I told him I didn't mind hanging out, but I wanted to make it clear that I did not want it to be a date. He said he understood.

Then, a few days later, I got sick. It started off with what I thought was just a bad cold, but it kept escalating. I was awake the entire night shaking, cold, running a fever, and it hurt to swallow so much that it made me want to cry every time I did. I was getting dizzy and lightheaded and didn't want to get out of bed. I called off work one night and spent the entire day resting, drinking tea, and taking Nyquil. I wanted to call out again, but since I had called out the week before over a case of food poisoning, I didn't want to rack up the third point and get a reprimand. I was feeling a little better, so I chose to go to work. As soon as I got outside in the cold weather after the cast member meeting, it hit me like a brick. My manager, Raul, sent me home early. I did everything I could to try and feel better, but the next morning I felt worse. I was in bed, crying. I asked Tori to take me to the hospital. She told me that I would be fine and went to sleep. Then Landon came in and I asked him to take me. He agreed and brought me to urgent care, where I was diagnosed with tonsillitis. I got a doctor's note to avoid a reprimand and took the antibiotics they prescribed for me. The next day at work, I was still feeling under the weather, but still miles better than I was. I took my doctor's note to a manager and explained what had happened; however, I was told that because it wasn't two consecutive days that I called out, they wouldn't take it. All I could think was, 'So because I tried to be a good cast member and actually go to work, I'm being punished. Whereas if I hadn't tried at all, they would've accepted my note and I would be fine. Because that's fair.' I was worried about what this was going to mean for me staying as a cast member, but I tried to shake it off.

I was off for two days after that, and when I came back to work the third day, I was called into Kathleen's office. She was the leader who had refused to take the doctor's note, and now she was giving me the reprimand. She apologized and told me that she felt like I didn't deserve it, but it was just the way the system went. I talked to her for a while—she was one of my favorite managers, and I valued her opinion. I was feeling terrible about the reprimand and how it might affect me staying at Disney. While she couldn't dispel my fears, she did tell me something that will stay with me forever:

> I'm my own worst critic. There's nothing that any of you can tell me about myself that I don't already know. That's why I've learned not to measure myself by how many times I've failed or fallen short, but by the number of times that I pick myself back up and keep going. You could give up at any time, or you can get up and keep trying. When you look back you'll see that those were your real successes. You can always turn something that was a potential loss into a win. If you can't change your situation, change your mind set. Make the most out of wherever you are.

Although I left the office in tears, I carried her words with me. Another manager, Peter, caught me on the way out and tried to comfort me by saying, "It doesn't mean it's the end of your Disney career. It might just be a small hiccup." I know he meant well, but I didn't feel much better. Justin walked me out to my car, which he conveniently parked alongside. I called my mom on the way out, crying, telling her about how I got a reprimand for trying to be a good cast member and now I might not get to stay. She could hear the panic in my voice and told me not to jump to conclusions yet, since we didn't know whether this would have any effect on my future. Justin could see how upset I was, and as he opened up his trunk said to me, "I wasn't going to give this to you until tomorrow, but I figured now would be a good time." He pulled out a stuffed animal of Baymax, from *Big Hero 6*. I cried even harder and held onto Baymax like hugging him would somehow make things better. I said goodbye to Justin, telling him I would see him in the morning. Tomorrow was that day of "hanging out" that we had planned.

Justin picked me up at 10am, greeting me with yellow roses, and took me to Downtown Disney. I had assumed that we were going to watch *Big Hero 6*, since he had just given me the Baymax doll, which I had brought with me, his little head and big white arms hanging out of my purse. There was time until the movie started, so we went to Starbucks first—although it was the last thing I wanted, as I was on day 3 of my antibiotics and my stomach wasn't happy to be receiving them. We watched *Big Hero 6*, an incredible movie that made my mascara run with tears. We then walked up and down Downtown Disney, looking through shops and talking. Later in the afternoon we decided to eat at Earl of Sandwich. Justin wouldn't let me pay, but I shook it off—and then, while we were eating, he reached into his back pocket and slapped two bright green Disney tickets down on the table.

"No way," I gasped, nearly dropping my sandwich.

"Yep."

"I thought they were sold out."

"That's just what I told you. Surprise!"

"Tonight?"

"Tonight."

"Can we go now?"

"If you want to," he laughed.

I was so excited I didn't even finish my sandwich. We were going to Mickey's Very Merry Christmas Party!

When we got into the car to go to the party, Justin informed me that he had brought a costume change and needed to switch shirts. As he started changing into a more formal, red button-up shirt, he said, "Oh, I have something else for you, too." He handed me a box from the back seat.

I stared at the box for a solid minute before opening it. A thousand thoughts raced through my mind when I read the words "Arribas Brothers". I knew which store this was, because we had just walked through it a few minutes before going to Earl of Sandwich. It was full of very expensive, very glittery, diamond gifts. I could only imagine what was in the box, although I didn't really want to see. Finally, I slowly opened the box, delicately pulling away the tissue paper, and found a beautiful princess crown. It was so stunning that it took my breath away. I held the crown delicately in my hands, afraid that if I did so much as breathe the wrong way I would damage its beauty. It had three big jewels on the front that reminded me of Rapunzel's crown, which made me love it even more. I don't know how long I was staring at the crown before I pulled myself together, and then I could think only one thing: "He definitely does not believe that this is just friends." Then I got worried, really worried. I was almost uncomfortable the rest of the night. Regardless, I tried to have as much fun as I could at the party. I bought a green Christmas Goofy sweater (I should say *he* bought it for me; I wasn't allowed to pay for anything). We got hot chocolate and cookies and watched the parade, which was great, but I was sad when my favorite Ice Cutter danced by because I missed Landon; our friendship just wasn't the same any more. We watched the fireworks from Liberty Square, and then went over to Storybook Circus so I could give my favorite Santa Goofy nose kisses.

Come the end of the night, Justin was upset. He said that he had done all this to impress me. It was an uncomfortable conversation to have, but I was interested only in being friends with him, and I had to stand by that despite the gifts. By the end of all of it, he understood and we remained friends.

There was someone who didn't understand, and that was, well, my entire apartment. I came home with Baymax, roses, and my crown in hand. Tori, Amanda, and Landon were on the couch with nothing to say about the story of my time with Justin. They just looked away and back at the TV. Thinking it was strange, I put the roses on the counter and went to my room to sleep. The next morning I woke up and found that Landon had left our matching keychain on the counter next to Justin's roses. I grabbed the keychain and threw it across the room at the wall, upset that I was losing him.

Nobody in my apartment spoke to me for days. Landon was always there, with Tori and Amanda, but none of them wanted anything to do with me, and I hadn't the slightest idea why. One night Jackie told me that she planned on having her boyfriend over that night, so I just went to Bobby's to stay the night, crashing on his couch after a long game of Disney Scene It? (which he destroyed me at, by the way).

The next night I was trying to sleep, and everyone was out in the living room being loud as ever. I heard rustling through the paper-thin walls, followed by the sound of Landon's voice laughing and saying, "You all know you wanted to do it!" Then the sound of Amanda's voice, "She's going to be so pissed!" I rolled over and threw a pillow on top of my head, I knew they were doing something to mess with me, but I wasn't going to deal with it right then. I was too tired.

Sure enough, the next morning I woke to a note in the sink saying, "Clean your disgusting mucus!" My heart was broken. That night, I confronted Landon, but it only turned into an embarrassing screaming match, and all he had to say was, "I don't care, I don't want to be around you right now. I don't want to talk to you, go away." I sat in my room and cried, not sure how I had gotten to this point with him.

The next day Landon came into my room and told me that he was upset with me because he thought that I had broken up Justin and his girlfriend. He also thought I was sleeping with a married man at work, for reasons that I still don't understand.

"I just don't like the decisions that you're making lately. You're being a homewrecker and I don't want to be friends with someone like that," he told me. "I think that you and I are just too different. I think that PAC and Entertainment are just very different departments." I tried to tell him that if he had talked to me at all over the last few weeks, he would know that none of these things were true. He only shrugged, and then told me that Tori and Amanda were mad at me because I was sick, and then went out with Justin two days later.

"Why do they care?" I asked

"They just think that it looks weird, because antibiotics don't work that fast."

"Yes they do," I argued, that's why they're a-n-t-i-b-i-o-t-i-c-s. Besides, it's my body, if I feel well enough to go out, I should be able to go out. They're not my mom."

"I'm just telling you how they feel," Landon said, and strutted out of the room.

That was the last real conversation I had with Landon. Just like that, because I got sick, my picture-perfect friendship with Landon and my roommates was over. I was losing my job at Disney. I felt the world I loved crash around me over what seemed like just a really bad cold. Before I gave up all hope, though, I printed off my resume and went to Casting to ask about transferring into a part-time or full-time role. The cast member at the desk took my perner (Disney ID) number, and 10 minutes later called me to her desk to let me know that I didn't meet transfer guidelines. I would have to exit the company for six months before applying again.

That's when the heartbreak really sunk in. I thought about how much I had sacrificed to participate in this program. I thought about my mom being in the hospital the day I left, I thought about all the magic that I made here with Brooke, with Bobby, the twins, Greg, Angie and Micheline, Kevin. I thought about Fantasmic! and being known as the Main Street Bubble Girl, and I could feel it all slipping through my fingers because I came to work one day instead of calling out. I tried hard not to be bitter, but between this, Landon, my roommates, and having to deal with the Christmas crowds every night, it was hard not to be.

One night Kevin stopped by the firehouse to get his Sorcerer cards, mentioning that he was happy to see that I was still here after all this time. Kevin had been my guest for almost a year now, and it was always a relief to see him come into town. I told him about my situation with having to leave the company for six months before I could come back, and I saw his bright blue eyes narrow. "That's ridiculous," he told me. "I know, but hey, man, you know I'll be back." This was Kevin's last trip of the year, and he was leaving the next day. He told me that he would come find me on the parade route before he left, but I never saw him. It crushed me that I didn't get to say goodbye to one of my favorite guests.

This whole thing was crushing me, but I kept Kathleen's words in the back of my mind, and despite not being able to stay with Disney, I chose to stay in Florida. After all I had worked for, I felt it was right that I stayed here. So I found an apartment that I could move into on December 2. I tried to keep it from my roommates, but it didn't last long. Amanda gave me attitude about it, saying, "I guess I'll just tell my mom to throw away the stocking she made you." But how could I have known that her mom was making me a stocking? Nobody in this apartment even talked to me.

One night I was walking around Vista Way, thinking about everything and trying to figure out what to do, when I ran into Jamie. I said hello, and amazingly, he said hello back. He must have seen the hurt on my face because he looked at me like he was concerned and asked what was wrong. I just apologized to him, over and over again, explaining that Landon had done to me what he did to Jamie. Even if I didn't realize at the time what Landon did to Jamie, I saw it now, and I understood why Jamie was so upset with us. I told him over and over how much I missed him, how I never wanted to hurt him, how much he meant to me. I told him that I would always think of him lying on the couch with me at the Patterson apartment watching YouTube videos. I was in tears talking to Jamie, but he didn't return the affection as strongly. He told me that he wanted to believe me, he wanted to believe that I was a good person, but he just wasn't sure yet. He said that he would consider giving me another chance. He came inside and we sat on my couch until three in the morning. He had really pulled himself together and was so much happier about everything since the last time I saw him. He had been accepted to his dream school in California and had moved up in the restaurant at the UK Pavilion. In general he looked happier, healthier, and I was so thrilled to see him that way. When he went to leave he gave me a hug, and I latched onto him, sobbing into his shoulder, begging for him to forgive me, to not let this be the last time he saw me, but it was. Despite my efforts to reach out to him for months afterward, he never responded and I never saw him again.

I moved out of Vista Way a week later and began moving into my new apartment. I had no furniture. Luckily, Becky was nice enough to let me borrow an air mattress until I could save the money to get a real bed. My roommates were Melissa, who worked at the Haunted Mansion and Jungle Cruise; Jordan, who worked the fireworks for

Fantasmic!; and Katelyn, who was a Kilimanjaro Safaris driver at Animal Kingdom. When I moved in Katelyn was out, but her friend Roberta was staying over. Roberta and I hit it off right away, sitting on the porch in the mornings drinking coffee and talking for hours. The other two roommates were very quiet and rarely left their rooms, but it was such a nice change from Vista. I could sleep at night without people screaming until four in the morning, and I had my own room. I was significantly happier already.

So then I began the job search. I spent several days camped out on the couch applying for as many jobs that I could possibly find, just praying that someone would hire me. I only had less than a month until my college program ended.

A few days later I went home for a week for a much-needed visit. My mom and aunt were graduating with their bachelor degrees, so I went back to watch them walk, and we had a miniature Christmas, seeing as I would be working on Christmas day. It was a more humble trip than the last one. I was happy to be home, I was happy to see the mountains and the open fields, I was happy to see everyone, and all of the cats. I thought about what it would be like to move back, and maybe it wouldn't be so bad. Despite everything that was going on, I was happy to be home again. While I was there, I got a call from Universal Studios, offering me an interview for a guest relations position that I had applied for. Things were looking up, and although it wasn't staying at Disney like I had always dreamed, I kept Kathleen's words at heart: "Make the most out of wherever I was."

When I got home from my trip, I had my interview. They were no longer hiring for guest relations, but I was offered a position bussing tables at The Three Broomsticks in Hogsmeade. The only condition was that they needed me to start right away; they weren't willing to wait until my program ended, and if I didn't accept the position, I would have to wait six months before I could re-apply to Universal. I went home from the interview and started throwing things against the walls. I didn't want to quit Disney early, but I had to pay rent. Reluctantly, I took the job, determined to try and work *both* until my program ended so I could complete this year successfully. It almost worked, too. Universal was scheduling me in the mornings and Disney at night. Granted, I was working 8am–2am and showing up to my shifts at Disney almost an hour late, but I was doing it.

I had one day off, and I chose to spend it in the Magic Kingdom doing my victory lap. I took my graduation ears that they gave us at the service celebration and got them embroidered with "Cami DCP 2014". I wore my best dress and heels and got lots of pictures taken. I said goodbye to my favorite Streetmosphere performer, the one who told Andrew and Alex to love me on my birthday. I teared up a little bit saying goodbye to her, but nothing was harder than when I went to say goodbye to Mickey.

"Hey, Mickey, I just finished my program. I came to say goodbye."

Mickey Mouse waved his arms yelling, "Congratulations!" and placed a hand on my arm saying "Aw I am so proud of you."

The sound of Mickey Mouse telling me that he was proud made me burst into tears.

"Thanks, Mickey." I managed to get out between sobs.

"So, what are you going to do after this?" Mickey asked.

I couldn't possibly tell him that I was going to Universal, but I did have other goals for my future, so I told him those. "Well, Mickey, I'm moving to Florida, so I'll be here, and now I just really want to find a way that I can help children with disabilities."

Mickey took a step closer, placing a hand on my shoulder and saying, "Aw, thank you, pal. That really means a lot."

I cried even more, and he asked to take a picture. We took a couple of photos and I wiped my eyes, telling him, "Thanks again, Mickey."

Mickey smiled and said, "Say, can I get one last hug?"

So I gave Mickey Mouse one more giant hug and went to leave. Mickey called after me: "See ya real soon!"

Chapter Fifteen

I left Town Square Theater sadder than ever. I sat down to take off my giant heels and noticed Mary Poppins on top of the train station, along with Mr. Penguin. I hadn't met Mr. Penguin yet, so I went up to say hello to them. I told Mary that I had just finished my program and I was sad to leave and she told me something that really changed my perspective on life: "You mustn't get too attached, you know. You should only ever promise to stay somewhere until the wind changes." I knew that she was right, and the words helped me to let go just a little more.

I kept on with trying to balance the two jobs, but by the end of an exhausting week, I got my new schedule for Universal and it overlapped with Disney almost every day. There was no way that I could pull it off. Disney scheduled me to work until 2 in the morning on Christmas, and my first day of on-the-job training at Universal was the very next day at 7am. I couldn't go into work that tired. I wouldn't have even slept if we're considering travel time.

So I worked the night of Christmas Eve, and then I called out of Disney on Christmas Day. The next morning I went to my first day of training "with the muggles" at Harry Potter, and as soon as my shift ended, I went home and gathered all my costumes, main gates, and IDs. Trying to turn off all emotion, I made my coffee the next morning and returned every costume I owned, except for one red bow tie. I couldn't resist. Then I went to the coordinator's office while I waited for the day parade to end. I tried to drown out the sound of "Once upon a Christmas time at Christmas" as I told Bill and Abe that I was there to self-term. Abe cried and gave me a hug goodbye, promising to come visit me as soon as he could. Bill did everything he could to cheer me up, noticing that I was wearing a shirt with a picture of Walt Disney, and said "The man on your shirt left for California with $10 in his pocket and all of this was the end result. You can do anything you set your mind to."

Bill will never understand how much those words meant to me. I carried them with me as I climbed the longest flight of stairs to the manager's office. I saw Kathleen and asked to speak with her. I shut the door to her office, which felt heavier than before, and sat down. I explained to her that the reprimand I had gotten for being sick had pushed me out of transfer guidelines, and the only job that I could find needed me now. I told her how tired I was from trying to work both and that I couldn't do it any more. I knew it was terrible to leave with only 2 ½ weeks left of my program, but it was either I leave now on a good note, or call out so much over the next 2 weeks that I really would destroy any chance that I had of ever coming back to the company.

Kathleen was more than understanding and comforting. She apologized that all of this happened to me, telling me that I didn't deserve it. She knew how much this place meant to me, how much I loved being here. "Disney will always be here for you when you come back," she told me, giving me a hug as I went to leave. I grabbed the doorknob and stopped, turning to face her again with tears rolling down my cheeks, "Hey, Kathleen, I know Tran doesn't come in until later, but when he does, will you just…" I couldn't make out any more words—my mouth had froze—but she already knew. "I will, Cami. I will." I put my head down for a moment and then said, "Thanks, Kathleen. I appreciate it." As I left her office, I walked past another manager, Ben, but I didn't say anything. I was too embarrassed about crying that I just kept walking. I went into the bathroom to fix my make-up before I left, and when I came out there was Jeff, telling me that Ben was looking for me. A moment later Ben came around the corner saying, "You didn't think I was going to let you leave without saying goodbye, did you?" He talked to me for a moment about how I can always come back to Disney, and how in the long run six months is such a short amount of time and it's a good opportunity for me to learn something new. Since I was at Universal, I could come back with dual park experience and have more to offer. He told me not to be discouraged, that Disney would always be there, and he knew I had plenty of friends with guest passes to get me into the parks to visit. "I just had to make sure I talked to you. There are some people that you just *have* to say goodbye to." He gave me a hug and I thanked him again, and was on my way.

The walk through the Utilidors from Town Square to the entrance at the back of Fantasyland is one mile, but that day it felt like five. The drive home is only 20 minutes, but it felt like hours. I was quite literally walking away from the world that I loved. I knew I would return as a guest, without a doubt. But maybe not as a cast member.

All I could do was to wait for the six months to pass. I was more or less enjoying working at Universal, though understanding now that post-Disney depression is a real thing. (I know of some CPs who have had to go to therapy after leaving Disney because it gets that bad.) I also learned that while Disney will do anything to make their guests happy, Universal treats their employees miles better than Disney treats theirs. Most people who worked at Universal came from Disney, and swore to never go back. But I wouldn't listen to them, still determined to return to the Magic Kingdom. As time went, on I was slowly pulling my life together outside of Disney, pending time on Thursdays with Becky and James, who often got me into the parks with their guest passes. I began a relationship with a wizard performer who I was working with, and I was volunteering on a regular basis at Give Kids the World. Eventually, I found an even better job at the Wyndham Orlando Resort as a guest service agent.

As soon as my six months of waiting were over, I wasted no time in applying for the Mouse. I landed an interview, and I walked through the long mural-painted walls of the Casting building as confident as ever and so, so ready to come back.

My interviewer wasted no time with small talk. She looked at her screen and asked "What happened during your College Program?" I explained to her every thing, the ups and the downs, and how it didn't feel right being in Florida away from my family, not doing what I came out here to do, and that I wanted nothing more than to come back.

She told me that they were not ready to forgive the reprimand from the end of my program, and that I would have to prove that I can hold one job for at least six months and not get terminated for attendance before they would consider hiring me again. "But even then, it's going to be hard for you because you're on a restricted rehire status."

Essentially, she told me to wait six more months and to try again later. It killed me. It was at that point I decided that I was done with Disney. I purchased an annual pass so I could visit the parks whenever

I wanted, but as far as being a cast member, I lost interest. It took me forever to stop being bitter over the situation, to stop hating Disney. For months I griped about how I couldn't stand the company and how despite all I had left behind and given up to work for them, they left me in the dirt. The more I came out about what had happened, the more I heard about similar things happening to other former CPs. I finally just let it go, and despite all my frustrations about how things ended, I will always swear by the College Program and how it changed my life. I would do it all again in a heart beat.

As far as everyone else:

- Harrison moved back from Texas. We rekindled our friendship and often visit Sea World together.

- Alyx came back, too, for a second program. A lot of people returned for second and third college programs.

- One day while I was visiting the parks waiting to meet Tiana, I saw Kevin in line to get his sorcerer's cards. It was the first time I had seen him since the night in the firehouse in December. He was ecstatic to see me, giving me a hug and saying that he thought he was never going to see me again.

- I still see the Silly Hat Sunday girls when I visit the parks.

- The twins have come down to visit twice since they left in August, and our friendship is stronger than ever.

- Greg and Rachel just celebrated their one-year anniversary. Greg hasn't come back to Orlando to visit yet, but he plans on doing so soon.

- Bobby and I finally decided to cut our losses, stop fighting, and stop talking.

- Jessica and Adam are coming back for another program.

- Legs is still with her boyfriend, and Veronica is getting married.

- Vince and I are still best friends, and we plan to become room-mates at the beginning of next year.

Chapter Sixteen

Life is moving on, and I'm learning that while post-Disney depression is definitely a thing, life without Disney is not. No matter where I end up, I will carry the experiences from my program with me forever.

I officially became a cast member onJanuary 24, 2014, and my last day of work was December 24, 2014, eleven months to the day. Eleven months of magic, misery, adventure, challenge, heartbreak, happiness, friendship, and experience. Eleven months that changed my life. Eleven months of fireworks, of characters, of Mickey Mouse and Tinkerbell. Eleven months of the Main Street Electrical Parade. Eleven months of Wishes. Eleven months of creating happiness for my guests, guests that I loved, guests that I will never forget.

I think about myself as a child, when my grandparents took me to Disneyland at 9 years old. We were sitting on the sidewalk waiting for the parade to start when I looked at my grandmother and told her, "I'm going to work here someday." Later, when we were waiting in line for Indiana Jones, a cast member came up to my grandmother pointing at her shirt and said, "Hey, you have Pooh on your shirt." My grandmother panicked until remembering that she was wearing a shirt that had Winnie the Pooh on it. In that moment I knew that I wanted to be that cast member who told terrible Disney jokes.

I've held on to those dreams since that day, and I made them happen. I realized it the day that I was exhausted from heat and life when I saw a girl on the parade route wearing a pair of Glow with the Show Ears. I ran up to her almost in a panic, asking her, "Oh, my gosh, ma'am are you okay? Are you sure you're feeling alright? You look a little light headed!" (Get it? *Light*-headed? Because it's, yeah, okay, you get it.)

I hope that 9-year-old Cami is proud that we made our dreams come true. Although my time at Disney is over, I know that after everything I've done and been through during my program, all the magic I've made and the memories I've created, the sights I've seen and the people I've met, after all of it, I can finally say: Cami Earned Her Ears.

About the Author

Cami Scovotti grew up in Loveland, Colorado, and was going to school in Fort Collins, Colorado, for Hospitality Management, concentrating in Hotel Management. However, after working with the Make-A-Wish families at Disney and volunteering at Give Kids the World as a character performer, she discovered her passion for helping children with disabilities, and so will be returning to Colorado to pursue a degree in Occupational Therapy at Colorado State University in Fort Collins.

More Books from Theme Park Press

Theme Park Press publishes dozens of books each year for Disney fans and for general and academic audiences. Here are just a few of our titles. For the complete catalog, including book descriptions and excerpts, please visit:

ThemeParkPress.com

Sara

EARNS HER EARS

My Secret Walt Disney World Cast Member Diary

SARA LOPES
Earning Your Ears: Volume Three

Katie

EARNS HER EARS

My Secret Walt Disney World Cast Member Diary

KATIE HUDSON
Earning Your Ears: Volume Four

Brittany

EARNS HER EARS

My Secret Walt Disney World Cast Member Diary

BRITTANY DICOLOGERO
Earning Your Ears: Volume Five

Two Girls and a Mouse Tale

Elly and Caroline Collins

Disneyland SECRETS

GAVIN DOYLE

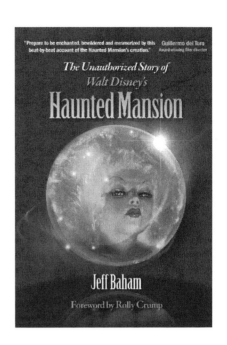

"Prepare to be enchanted, bewildered and mesmerized by this beat-by-beat account of the Haunted Mansion's creation." — Guillermo del Toro, Award-winning film director

The Unauthorized Story of Walt Disney's

Haunted Mansion

Jeff Baham

Foreword by Rolly Crump

THE

RIDE DELEGATE

Memoir of a Walt Disney World VIP Tour Guide

Annie Salisbury

MURDER

IN THE MAGIC KINGDOM

Annie Salisbury

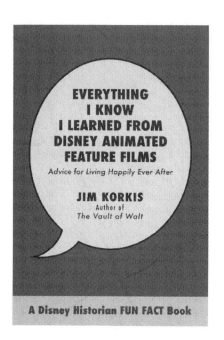

EVERYTHING
I KNOW
I LEARNED FROM
DISNEY ANIMATED
FEATURE FILMS
Advice for Living Happily Ever After

JIM KORKIS
Author of
The Vault of Walt

A Disney Historian FUN FACT Book

D
is for
Disneyland
THE UNOFFICIAL KIDS' GUIDE TO
THE HAPPIEST PLACE ON EARTH
Kelly Pope Adamson

"I SAW ARIEL DO A KEG STAND"
The WILD Side of Walt Disney World

CHRIS GRIMM

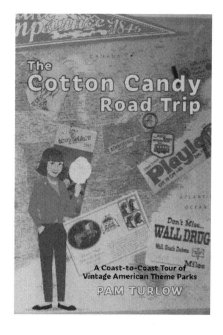

The
Cotton Candy
Road Trip

A Coast-to-Coast Tour of
Vintage American Theme Parks
PAM TURLOW

77879008R00075

Made in the USA
Columbia, SC
28 September 2017